Barbaralee Diamonstein

Interior
DESIGN

The New Freedom

Ward Bennett
Robert Bray and Michael Schaible
Mario Buatta
Angelo Donghia
Joseph Paul D'Urso
Mark Hampton
Warren Platner
John F. Saladino
Robert A.M. Stern
Sarah Tomerlin Lee
Lella and Massimo Vignelli
Introduction by Paul Goldberger

RIZZOLI
NEW YORK

Published in the United States of America in 1982 by
RIZZOLI INTERNATIONAL PUBLICATIONS, INC
712 Fifth Avenue, New York, NY 10019

Interior Design: The New Freedom is based on a series of
edited interviews conducted by Barbaralee Diamonstein at the
New School for Social Research/Parsons School of Design
in New York.

LC 82-50501
ISBN 0-8478-0445-3

Designed by Massimo Vignelli

Set in type by University Graphics, Inc.
Printed and bound by Arti Grafiche Amilcare Pizzi, S.p.A.,
Milan, Italy

Library of Congress Cataloging in Publication Data

Diamondstein, Barbaralee.
  Interior design, the new freedom.

  1. Interior decorators—United States—Interviews.
2. Interior decoration—United States—History—20th
century. I. Title.
NK2004.D5   1982   729   82-50501
ISBN 0-8478-0445-3

Contents

Art.
NK
2004
D5
1982

For Louise Nevelson and Carl Spielvogel
whose grand designs
have embellished my life

Today, not much freedom remains for individual self-expression. Among the notable exceptions, however, is the design of one's own surroundings. This is true to such a considerable extent that interior design has come to serve as an indicator of education, class role and social status, a tip-off to the inhabitant's occupation as well as his preoccupations, and a pretty fair guide to his personality as well. Design has always been subject to the tides of fashion; now, more than ever, it is a barometer of our life and times.

Previous centuries celebrated the work of the best cabinet-makers, upholsterers and architects in cathedrals and palaces. Modern interior design, which synthesizes architecture and craftsmanship, incorporates all of those forms but now it does so in people's homes, not in grand palazzos or elaborate places of worship.

The powerful influence of interior design in our day is all the more striking when we consider that, a century ago, it was not even dimly recognized as a distinctive discipline. But in 1897, with the publication of *The Decoration of Houses*, by the novelist Edith Wharton and Ogden Codman Jr., interior design was at last deemed a worthwhile undertaking. As the authors emphasized, no comparable study of "house-decoration as a branch of architecture" had been printed in England or the United States for at least fifty years. "Various influences have combined," the authors wrote, "to sever the natural connection between the outside of the modern house and its interior. In the average house, the architect's task seems virtually confined to the elevations and floor-plan. The designing of what are today regarded as insignificant details, such as mouldings, architectraves, and cornices, has become a perfunctory work, hurried over and unregarded; and when this work is done, the upholsterer is called in to 'decorate' and furnish the rooms." For too long, said Wharton and Codman, people had merely been piling up gaudy, complicated ornament and superficial effects; instead of concentrating on adornment, the authors urged, architects and decorators should pay heed to the alterations of spatial properties, guided by common sense and a respect for simplicity. In fact, the book's discussion of the structural proportions of the home became a significant influence on the first generation of professional interior decorators.

Even before Wharton and Codman issued their manifesto on the designer's art, the industrial revolution had set the stage for some major developments by bringing about a general increase in education and leisure time. The twentieth century brought a number of other changes, in esthetics, technology and the growing appeal of the designer's work. Soon after the turn of the century, along came such grandes dames of decoration as Elsie de Wolfe, Ruby Ross Wood and Syrie Maugham, women who cultivated and promoted a "modern" sensibility in the design of the home. Intelligent, well bred and widely traveled, these pioneers with no architectural training, established themselves as decorators when such a term barely existed.

When the flamboyant Elsie de Wolfe set up business in 1905, American homes were largely functional, if not drab, affairs stuffed with memorabilia and reflecting the country's obsession with Victoriana and humorless revivals of European periods. De Wolfe launched nothing less than a revolution in American home decoration with her vision of "good taste," emphasizing uncluttered yet comfortable rooms. Echoes of that revolution reverberate even today, in the esthetic espoused by so many modern designers. "My business," wrote De Wolfe in 1917, "is to preach to you the beauty of suitability. Suitability! *Suitability! SUITABILITY!* It's such a relief," she continued, "to return to the tranquil, simple forms of furniture, and to decorate our rooms by a process of elimination. How many rooms have I not cleared of junk—this heterogenous mass of ornamental 'period' furniture and bric-a-brac bought to make a room 'look cozy.' Once cleared of these, the simplicity and dignity of the room comes back, the architectural spaces are freed and now stand in their proper relation

Barbaralee Diamonstein

Foreword

to the furniture. In other words, the architecture of the room becomes its decoration." Rumored to be the first to dye her hair violet, to stand on her head for the sake of fitness and to dance the foxtrot, she was also the first to make decoration "glamorous." Her eclectic rooms included furniture of different periods, flowered-chintz slipcovers and the draped skins of leopards and zebra.

Georgia-born Ruby Ross Wood took comfort rather than suitability as the governing idea behind all her designs. A journalist *(Vogue, House & Garden)* turned decorator, Wood in 1918 established the first decorating department, "Au Quatrième," in New York's Wanamaker's Department Store. Almost as famous for her wit and charm as for the originality of her designs and her color-drenched rooms, she is reputed to have told a client who approached her with two suggestions for decorating a house: "We will consider only the one that is most comfortable."

Third and last of the pioneers was Syrie Maugham, who in 1922 began to exert her influence from London, where she was the first to assemble all-white rooms. According to the decorator Billy Baldwin, Maugham's trademark designs had "every bit as much vitality and drama as rooms that were multicolored—and twice the romance." Maugham not only initiated the use of the white sheepskin or carved-wool carpet; she included in her interiors variations in texture (satin and velvet to chintz, fur and wool) and in monotones (the natural grainy white of linen and muslin to frosty snow white and blond, bleached wood).

Many decorators of this age were less concerned with creating an environment to their own tastes than with taking a client's furniture and other objects and making them work in the space that was available. Some designers, such as Vanessa Bell and Duncan Grant, helped to sweep away altogether the convention of using "period" pieces. During the 1920s and '30s, they created handpainted murals and original designs for carpets, wallpaper, fireplaces and furniture, and helped invigorate the languishing decorative arts tradition in this country. The influence of such "decorators" peaked between the wars. It was largely as a result of their example that honeymooners during this period began to redecorate their living spaces with "individuality" and a "modern" style of living in mind.

If these early decorators were preoccupied with style rather than economy or feasibility, a very different attitude was evolving across the ocean, one that would also have considerable impact on today's ideas about interior design. At the Bauhaus, the notion of the "complete building" was taking hold, embracing architecture, sculpture and painting and inspiring designers from the 1930s to the present. Walter Gropius, Mies van der Rohe and Marcel Breuer were among those architects whose brilliant investigations into new spatial forms and achievements in the use of machine-crafted materials helped bring about the most extensive changes ever in the design of our interiors.

With these influences, design became a more and more deliberate composition, founded on technical training as well as esthetic sense. "Sister" Parish, Billy Baldwin and other inheritors of the design tradition combined a natural sense of taste and style not only with extensive knowledge of periods and materials but also with sound business sense. Householders of the 1920s, '30s and '40s were awed by luxury and all things Continental, and were only too willing to be shown what was "correct." For this reason, a very set and visible "mainstream" esthetic began to emerge, presided over by one designer or another who dictated what *the* style should be.

By the 1950s and '60s, a change in terminology reflected a shift in orientation: what had been called "decoration" became "interior design." That terminology remains in use today, when the growing limitations of space and budget have persuaded client was well as designer to give equal priority to beauty and practicality. Now designers are prone to stress the redefinition and structural reorganization of a space as much as its decoration.

9

Because there is no longer a reigning designer who issues dictates for all to follow, today's designers must work more closely with each client, divining his or her personal needs and preferences. Most of the designers with whom I spoke emphasized the paramount importance of their relationship with the client. "I don't like a client who just says yes, and doesn't know the difference between a good idea and a bad idea," says Mark Hampton. Ward Bennett concurs: "I do not take a client unless we can have something that could be compared to a marriage—where one can really learn to like the other, and neither makes any final decisions relating to furniture and accoutrements." Says Mike Schaible: "The ideal client is one you really become involved with in the project." Many designers made clear their conviction that the sophistication of the American public is greater than ever, which makes the designer-client collaboration increasingly effective—and important.

Interior designers today must be concerned not just with assembling furniture, fabrics and rugs from various vendors, but with creating a total environment. They assume the roles of architect, engineer and furniture-maker as well as that of the traditional decorator. In so doing they seek not simply to enhance space with ornamentation but actually to redefine space.

The backgrounds of today's designers are diverse. Ward Bennett was a designer of bridal gowns at the age of thirteen; John Saladino, who began as a promising painter, came to design "through the want ads"; Mark Hampton was educated at the London School of Economics; Sarah Tomerlin Lee started in magazine journalism, advertising and promotion. Some, such as Angelo Donghia, Mario Buatta, Bob Bray and Mike Schaible, knew from the time when they were quite young that they were destined for decoration. From them we hear stories of "moving the furniture around" in their parents' stores or living rooms. Some, of course, such as Robert A. M. Stern, Massimo and Lella Vignelli and Warren Platner, were trained as architects.

These conversations reflect the transformation that interior design has undergone since the turn of the century, even in the last two decades. But precisely how should it be described—as decoration, as interior design, as space planning? According to Angelo Donghia, the designer/decorator controversy serves to undermine the profession when, after all, the two functions are not all that dissimilar. Says Joseph Paul D'Urso: "It's irrelevant, as far as I'm concerned. It's the quality and the result that really matter." Ward Bennett asserts that, no matter what the profession is called, the fundamental job of a designer is to assist the client in creating a very personal "sense of place."

Rigid terminology is, in fact, no longer relevant. What does matter is flexibility, scrupulous attention to detail and each designer's highly personal esthetic signature. In these interviews, a number of distinct philosophies emerge, ranging from the traditional historical approach to novel "post-modernism." Most of the designers are engaged in either a penetrating examination of the past or a self-conscious experimentation with new materials and ideas; the pages of today's design magazines are proof enough that designers are divided between a love of the old and a dream of the new. This division, in turn, must be adapted to the specific needs of each client.

These conversations, part of the Van Day Truex Memorial Lecture Series at the New School/Parsons School of Design, were held before an audience in the spring of 1981. They were a logical progression from a number of other interviews that I conducted with artists, architects and photographers, focusing most recently on those who affect the visual and built environment: *Inside New York's Art World* (conversations with leading artists, critics, museum directors and gallery owners); *American Architecture Now* (conversations with widely-known architects); and *Visions & Images: American Photographers on Photography* (conversations with distinguished photographers). For their help in transforming this project into a reality, my thanks to the innovative dean of the Parsons School of Design, David Levy, to my able and resilient assistants, Jean Zimmerman and Jill Shaffer, and to Jack Healy, Judith Bressler and David Gordon of ABC Arts. All the interviews were videotaped by the ABC Arts network, and their transcripts have been made available by being placed with the Columbia University Oral History Archives. In the transition from oral to written form, of course, the transcripts have been condensed somewhat and edited for clarity. It is my hope that these interviews, whether on tape or in print, will prove an important addition to the growing literature of this growing field.

We hear so much about the self-indulgence of interior design, about the extravagances and excesses of both designers and clients, that it is comforting to be reminded that design involves discipline. One cannot come away from this series of conversations between Barbaralee Diamonstein and interior designers without this pleasing sense—without the realization, that is, that design is a serious business. But it is Barbaralee Diamonstein's special ability to be able to get these professionals to talk of the serious and difficult side of their profession without coming off as too serious themselves; most of them tend to be pleasant more than preachy, and if there is anything that should be said of the form of these conversations at the outset, before we even think of their content, it is that they read more easily than such things might ever be expected to.

The substance of these conversations does not add up to a neat, easily packaged summary of the directions in which interior design is moving at this moment. There is surely a sense of freedom; whether this is something new, as the title tells us, or whether it is just a tendency to mix different kinds of design, different esthetic approaches which were heretofore kept quite separate, is a question worth asking. In any case there is something in the air right now that was not there a decade ago, and these conversations help to clarify it. Few grapple directly with the mood of the moment, but this is as it should be, for *zeitgeists*, such as they are, do not move toward us like bulls which can be attacked head on. They are common senses, impulses which are broadly shared, but which take somewhat different forms in each artist who responds to them. The designers who speak in these pages wisely avoid defining the temper of the time too precisely—but through their words a sense of what it is nonetheless communicates itself to us.

My own view is that this is a moment of rather exhilarating confusion in interior design as it is in architecture. History, or historical styles, spurned by the serious as decadent or, worse still, as middlebrow, command new respect; a Louis XIV chair or a Chippendale highboy are not things that designers who think of themselves as shapers of our culture are likely to disdain now as they did less than a generation ago. Ornament, pattern, curtains, a profusion of objects— these are all things we once associated with conservatism, yet now it is the leaders of the profession who seem to talk of them.

In architecture, this constitutes a revolution of sorts— orthodox modernism toppled from its throne. In interior design, the picture is more complicated. Some designers, like Mario Buatta, have not changed at all—they have merely watched as what we might call highly studied architectural taste has come around to their way of seeing the world. The movement of an architect like Robert A. M. Stern toward an acceptance, even an active use of, traditional elements in interiors is also an indication of this. But others, designers like Joseph Paul D'Urso, Bob Bray and Mike Schaible, not to mention Ward Bennett, Warren Platner and Massimo and Lella Vignelli, are clearly working in what must be called the modernist tradition, the very stream of development that the avant-garde among architects appears to be putting aside.

There are a number of things going on here, and it is important to separate out the strands of meaning behind this seemingly topsy-turvy situation, this world in which it would appear that to be modern one must be conservative, and to be conservative one must be modern. First, the essential impulse of this time is a pluralistic one—we seem to believe, as we become a more visually concerned culture, that there is no single style appropriate to the moment. We do not, except in rare cases, attach moral values to styles—there is no sense that to be modern is to be pure, as there was at the Bauhaus, and it goes without saying that there is no sense that to be Gothic or classical is to embrace the values of either the Church or the Romans.

How, then, are stylistic choices made? Often on the basis

Introduction

Paul Goldberger

of emotional content or loose association; we can see that clearly in these conversations, as Angelo Donghia talks of his desire to make people "feel better," or as Mark Hampton tells us of his childhood fantasies of life among the rich. In each case, however, the designers here eschew quick and glib connections—they do not prance from Colonial Williamsburg to French Provincial, but endeavor to deal responsibly with the basics that underlie any stylistic choice—proportion, form, color, light, materials.

Now, the best interior designers (or decorators, as they once preferred to be called) always knew this, but one senses that it is being felt on a broader basis right now. And this calls forth the second crucial characteristic of this moment—a blurring of the line between architecture and design. Not long ago architects believed they made spaces and decorators filled them up; now each profession seems to like to do the work of the other, and is turning out to be good at it, too. Thus the turning upside down of modernism and revivalism: the modernist esthetic, which was long a kind of private, high-design province of architects and certain very special clients, has been brought by designers into a wider sphere of our culture. It has trickled down, in a sense, from architects to designers—at the same time that many perceptions of designers have begun to trickle up.

That the waters separating architecture from interior design have become so shallow and easily forded comes, in part, from the rapid increase in what we might call the visual consciousness of our culture. Objects are terribly important to us right now; we seem to want to use possessions, and hence a kind of visual literacy, as the means of establishing the social status that verbal literacy once offered. Architects alone cannot satisfy this social craving; neither could the small cadre of traditional, old-line decorators. It is no surprise, then, that a generation of excellent interior designers, merging the architect's sophistication with space with the decorator's connoisseurship of the object, could arise.

Curiously, the designers whose words fill these pages have varying ideas as to their profession's relationship to the society it both serves and molds, and they speak frankly to Barbaralee Diamonstein on this subject. Warren Platner, for one, comes off as deferential—more accommodating in his words, perhaps, than in his designs themselves. The designer's task "is to be serving people's needs, and he should not be imposing his psychological views on other people," he says, and follows with a plea for deep involvement on the part of his clients.

Angelo Donghia, who comes off as both a shrewd businessman and an engaging storyteller, says, "People want your advice, but they want you to tell them what they're thinking they want"—an indication, in a simple sentence, of his remarkable mix of marketing skill and design sense. The partners Bob Bray and Mike Schaible, whose minimalist work is sleek and sophisticated, come across as not a little demanding—they have a clear and definite idea of what they want to do, and their work is presented almost as a challenge to the client to live up to it.

This is not true of every designer who works in this style. Joseph Paul D'Urso speaks quite earnestly, even movingly, of his belief that we can improve life by editing it down to a few special things; he comes off as what we might call a humane minimalist, and he is the only designer in this book who is able to toss off a remark like, "I think we need beautiful windows, I really do," and not sound at all disingenuous. But not so different is D'Urso's mentor, Ward Bennett, whose narrative of his own career becomes the story of an entire life. Bennett talks of sources from Sir John Soane to Luis Barragan; he emerges as a man both canny and wise, and we learn as much about design in general from him as we might from a dozen books.

Ward Bennett's graciousness is contrasted with John Saladino's rather stand-offish posture—"I don't recognize interior design as an applied art but as a fine art," Saladino tells us, and then, "I don't care about the chair in terms of its

13

chairness, I'm concerned with it as an abstract shape." Ironically, Saladino's furniture is quite comfortable and his rooms are often inventive and handsome—far more accommodating than his rhetoric.

Mario Buatta, a designer of strong imprint and considerable talent, appears here as articulate, practical and kind. He denies that his work has hallmarks—"I'd like to think that it looked as though the people had some help but they, rather than one person, did it," he says. And this, too, may be more an indication of personality than of the actual facts of the matter—for here again the words of the designer, illuminating as they are, are not the best description of the work.

Robert A. M. Stern is characteristically incisive, devoting himself largely to a discussion of the failures of the modern movement in the making of interiors, and Sarah Tomerlin Lee, the hotel designer, turns out to be a savvy merchandiser indeed, but conscientiously concerned with finding ways to bring some decent design to the commercial marketplace. Equally enlightening is the conversation with Massimo and Lella Vignelli, whose remarkable design office ranges far and wide in its production of household objects and graphics as well as interiors. Massimo Vignelli speaks strongly about his growing realization that good design cannot, on its own, transform society; this admission is an important moment in these conversations, for it is not the kind of remark every designer is likely to make casually to every interviewer. It is one of the strengths of this book that this remark comes across not as despondent but almost as liberating. For there is a realism at the base of all of these interviews—a consciousness of the world as it is, and a celebration of attempts to make it better.

14

BLDD: *At various times, Ward Bennett has been a fashion illustrator and designer, a sculptor, a jewelry and tableware designer and an influential teacher. For the last thirty years, we've known him best as the distinguished designer of interiors and their furnishings. Ward, how did you come to excell in so many areas of design?*

WB: I left home when I was very young and got my first job in New York as a shipping clerk in the ladies' garment fabric business. I worked at that for about a year. Being exposed to designers, I naturally became interested.

BLDD: *Your formal education ended when you left grammar school—and home—at the age of thirteen. How and where did you live?*

WB: I lived at 124th Street and Broadway in a furnished room. And I worked for a firm called Chin-Chin Crêpe, wrapping and delivering fabrics.

BLDD: *Hand delivering?*

WB: Oh yes, in a two-wheeled hand truck. In fact, one of the most harrowing experiences in my life was delivering a whole truckload of bolts of fabric to B. Cohen, a lingerie company at Twenty-ninth Street and Madison Avenue. When I was trying to get the truck up onto the sidewalk on the southeast corner of Thirty-third Street, it went over.

BLDD: *Do you still pass there, and cringe?*

WB: Yes. *Everyone* out of *every* building was looking at me.

BLDD: *I assume that was a brief job. Was the incident the end of your employment there?*

WB: That was the end of the job.

BLDD: *Where did you go from there?*

WB: I had taken eight or ten lessons in fashion sketching from a woman called Madame Jeanette. Having met fashion designers when I was delivering the fabrics, I wanted to be one, too. So I walked up to Saks and spoke to a woman for whom I later worked at I. Magnin in San Francisco, Mademoiselle de Clair. I showed her my drawings and she thought they were interesting, so she gave me a job doing bridal sketches for the windows.

BLDD: *What did you know about brides and bridal sketches at age fourteen?*

WB: I was just doing sketches, I wasn't doing the original designs. They would show me a dress, hang it up, put it on a model, and then I would draw the garment for the display in the window.

BLDD: *Did that lead to other fashion illustration jobs?*

WB: No, I lasted there just two or three weeks, and then took a job at Franklin Fifth Avenue for another two weeks. Then I landed a very good job where I lasted for almost a year, working for Jo Copeland as a sketcher. When I left there, I worked at a few firms, Florscheimer and some others. Then, at about age fifteen and a half, I got my first job on my own, as a full-time designer.

BLDD: *What were you designing?*

WB: I designed the whole collection for a company called Joanne Juniors, owned by the Zinn brothers. At about age sixteen, they sent me to Europe to see the collections.

BLDD: *What did you discover while you were there? Did you discover enough to remain?*

WB: No. I came back and I was not recognizable: I went over on the *Queen Mary* and came back on the *Normandy*—with a mustache, a trench coat, a porkpie hat, riding britches and an English accent!

BLDD: *You've told me that your father was what is described as a "Dutch comedian" who specialized in dialect.*

WB: Yes, he was a vaudevillian.

BLDD: *So accents came to you easily. There you were, an English Ward Bennett. What did you do then?*

WB: I stayed with that firm for another two months or so, and then I went to California. I couldn't get a job, but I knew the people at Bullock's in Los Angeles. A few of them had worked at Bergdorf Goodman in New York. Then I got a job at I. Magnin in San Francisco that was doing windows more than fashion.

16

Ward Bennett

BLDD: *Designing windows, then, was one of your first moves toward interior design.*

WB: But I remained in fashion for another few years; I worked at Hattie Carnegie for four years. In fact, I was the costume designer for *Lady in the Dark*, with Gertrude Lawrence.

BLDD: *You did her costumes? What were they like?*

WB: One of the most famous was a little sequined vest. I remember it very well. And then we did all her personal costumes. Hattie Carnegie was well known at that time; Norell was working there, too. Carnegie was known not only as a designer for the social ladies of the world, but also for a great deal of theater—right up and down the line. Movie stars, too.

BLDD: *How did you come to meet Hattie Carnegie?*

WB: That was an interesting experience. I had come from California, and I went to see her. I didn't want to go back to Seventh Avenue. I knew this was *the* deluxe fashion house in New York—more so than Bergdorf Goodman. It was three or four townhouses on Forty-ninth Street. I showed her some sketches and also some muslins. By that time I had learned to cut muslins. And she said, "I'm sorry, but I don't need you. No, no, we have six designers—Bruno and Norell and Pauline Rothschild Potter, and so on." I said, "All right, let me work for you for nothing. Your windows are impossible. No one has done them in years. I don't want a penny. Just give me a month, give me two months." And she said, "Okay."

BLDD: *Let's get back to your interior design. As I recall, it was someone called Harry Jason who provided you with your first opportunity. How did that come about?*

WB: I'm sorry, I have to digress again. While I was at Carnegie, I studied at night with Hans Hofmann for two years.

BLDD: *Was that the period that you were at the Sculpture Center as well?*

WB: That's right. I worked with Louise Nevelson, downtown on Eighth Street. We shared a basement there.

BLDD: *Was this when you were both working in ceramics?*

WB: Exactly. And through that work in the mid-'30s, I got a job for Skidmore, Owings & Merrill doing four sculptures at the Terrace Plaza Hotel in Cincinnati. At the same time, Saul Steinberg and Alexander Calder were hired. I think I did that before I did the Harry Jason penthouse.

BLDD: *You were defining yourself more and more, at that point, as an artist, moving from illustration to painting to sculpture.*

WB: Right. At the same time I was doing the penthouse I was working with Hofmann, and also starting to sculpt; I introduced my clients to art. Mrs. Jason was my sister-in-law's sister. They had a lot of money and a penthouse at 945 Fifth Avenue, and they were not familiar with the arts. As I had been studying with Hofmann and had bought my first Picasso drawings, which at that time were about seventy-five dollars apiece, I was able to help them and guide them to buy very important works—African art, Picasso, Léger, Klee, Miró. These artists were then just beginning to be collected.

BLDD: *What did the furnishings look like in that first apartment?*

WB: Not dissimilar to what I'm doing today, oddly enough.

BLDD: *Can you recall and describe them?*

WB: It was a two-bedroom apartment with a maid's room, dining room, living room and a terrace on Fifth Avenue. I still feel that the most important thing is the architecture—the planning of the space, the actual circulation of the space. Utilities, kitchen, baths, storage, lighting, furniture are secondary. I took the terrace and did a glass greenhouse on it. Immediately, the living room became a greenhouse. So it was the space that started it all off. And then I did a built-in banquette. All the floors were cork; one wall of the foyer extended right through the living room. At the end there were double sliding doors to the dining room where there were books and objects from floor to ceiling. It was beautifully lit by Edison Price, who is still my mentor. That sort of working concept, I think, still exists today.

17

BLDD: *You still use cork, and those other materials, as well as some of those ideas?*

WB: Oh, sure. There was a white lacquer bookcase unit, all adjustable, all beautifully lit with low-voltage lighting. And then we began to collect. They made the choices—really beautiful things. That was the beginning of giving the apartment a personality, making it a meaningful place. I wouldn't live there; it wasn't for me. It was too elegant, too dressy, too formal. We had a yellow damask bedspread with a Scalamandré fringe around it, in a very modern room, and white *shoji* glass sliding into the walls overlooking the park, and a wall of mirror in the dressing room, a three-way mirror, and so forth—exactly what a lady of the house would need.

BLDD: *What problems in particular were presented to you by this being your very first job? Whatever your good intentions and good taste, very little experience went with it.*

WB: Don't forget, I had done window display for years. It's all linked—like working with objects and doing ten windows every ten days. I had worked at sculpting and painting and I'd made jewelry. I showed my jewelry at the Museum of Modern Art. And while I was working in ceramics with Nevelson, I showed in the Whitney Annual. I was working in various materials, and also associating, at this time, with interesting people. So, though I didn't have a formal education, my education came through my environment. When I was studying with Hofmann, I stayed at his house for two summers, on Cape Cod, in Provincetown.

BLDD: *What particular influence did Hofmann have on you and your work? One thinks of Hofmann as having a striking palette—and that is one thing we do not associate with you.*

WB: Hofmann did not force anything upon you. What I learned from him was the actual handling of space. He'd set up a still life and we would all draw it in black and white charcoal. This was merely to explore the tensions within that space. What pushed forward, what came toward you. Basically his big thought, his love, his poetry, was space; what was hap-

pening in space. And I've been dealing with that ever since.

BLDD: *How do you describe your work? What's the difference between a space, a place and a dwelling?*

WB: That's the most important question. First of all, if you are Parisian, that's your place. If you're a New Yorker, that's your place. I've just come from San Francisco; coming home to New York was not like going to Paris. So that's part of it: it's something personal, something meaningful, something that's me, not something purchased. I think that if I lived in Paris now exclusively, it would not be me. And I know Paris very well. So I think that's the beginning: with place. This is where contemporary interior design or architecture really fails.

BLDD: *Are you saying that they do not create a sense of place?*

WB: Exactly.

BLDD: *What are some of the most memorable places to you?*

WB: Georgia O'Keeffe's house, in New Mexico—the most undecorated, the most wonderful. A place, not just a space. Or Luis Barragan's house, Sir John Soane's house in London, Pompeii, the Sissinghurst Gardens.

BLDD: *All the places you mention as the most memorable to you are also the expression of very singular personalities, of extraordinary talents, of people who had a great awareness and concern for art, architecture, design, or all three. Not many of us have those gifts, or the opportunity to express them in that way.*

WB: I don't think a place has necessarily to be individually created. There are places—New York, in fact, is one—that create themselves. It can also happen in organic architecture. If you're living on a Greek island, you're going to get a beautiful house. Or if you're living in an adobe house, in Mexico. I think we have lost that sense of craft and of being part of the landscape, whether it is in New York or Milwaukee.

BLDD: *What are the greatest problems in the environments that you see today?*

WB: Often I cannot quite tell the difference between a resi-

18

Ward Bennett
Metal frame "Envelope" armchair
1960

dence and a showroom and a restaurant. They are all shiny and show-biz.

BLDD: *Too glossy for your taste?*

WB: Very glossy, and no personality. There's nobody there. As a matter of fact, recently I went to two apartments in the same evening, both done by a very, very well known designer in this area. The apartments were so similar in furniture, materials, even the art, that all you would have to do is change your clothes, and you wouldn't know whether you were in one apartment or the other.

BLDD: *You've described apartments that sound as if they are lacking in both grace and humor. Why is it all so serious? I'm not suggesting that interior design should be a sight gag. But if it's an environment for living, it seems to me there has to be some sense of play and some room for personality.*

WB: I think that is what's lacking. Very often the rooms we see—whether in Bloomingdale's, or *Architectural Digest*—are lacking in humor, and in art. And the art of living. Everything's set up, whether it's the table setting, or you name it. Even the towels are all peach and ochre.

BLDD: *How involved are your clients, and how early on in the process?*

WB: I like the client to be involved from the beginning. I do not take a client unless we really can have something that one could compare to a marriage—where one can really learn to like the other, and neither makes any final decisions relating to furniture and accoutrements.

BLDD: *One of the reasons that you're free to take on so few clients is because of the mass marketing of so many of your designs. It has permitted you the privilege of taking on only the clients that you want to. But you have an unusual way of working: you have no staff. How do you get along in that case? For example, who answers the phone? Who posts the mail?*

WB: I do have an assistant who worked for me as a draftsman at the firm Brickel Associates, which produces my furniture.

She works for me mornings answering the phone and doing the few letters. I have no other employees. My accountant comes once a month and does all the checks. And then I have a lawyer. That's it.

BLDD: *How did you manage to simplify your life so? It sounds like everyone's fantasy: to have a complicated work life—complicated, meaning productive, enriching and stimulating—and, on the other hand, an uncomplicated office life. Do you hire people on a free-lance basis?*

WB: Exactly. I've done four houses. If I need an engineer, I'll hire an engineer. If I need an architect, I'll hire an architect. If I need a draftsman, I'll hire a draftsman.

BLDD: *Do you get the best people to work for you in that way?*

WB: Oh, yes. People I've used for years. What I'm most successful at is living the way I do. I really mean that. I design interiors, and furniture, and flatware, and so forth. But I think the *way* I live is maybe the most meaningful.

BLDD: *You've designed a way of life, as well.*

WB: That's right. Very quiet, very uncomplicated, half the time in the country, a wonderful garden, a lot of travel. And all this doesn't require a lot of money. I've always done it. When I was seventeen, I took a year off and bicycled through France and stayed at youth hostels. And just this week I had a couple of lectures in San Francisco and Berkeley, and then took four days off and stayed in a cabin three hours north of San Francisco. Now, most people would rush the hell back to New York, but I won't do that.

BLDD: *How did that philosophy evolve so early on?*

WB: The three writers who have influenced me most in life are Thoreau, Whitman and Montaigne. I still read them; I have them at my bedside. This is also linked with Zen, of course—I mean, Lao Tzu—keeping it down to minimum. That relates to architecture—keeping down to a minimum, just simplifying.

BLDD: *Are you saying that our physical surroundings are just accoutrements to living life, and that the really grand design is life itself?*

WB: Indeed.

BLDD: *How have you managed to continue to free yourself to do more and better work?*

WB: I spend three or four days a week in the country, but of course, I'm always working. I have a kiln there and I also do collage. And I have two studios: a place in New York, at the Dakota, and then I have several other rooms where I can do my thinking. There's no phone; I can take a chair there or a piece of flatware or a glass or a dish or some new fabric to think about. I can be very cut off and quiet.

BLDD: *Let's talk for a moment about your "university chair" that you designed in the mid-1970s. How do you begin a design—do you start with models or drawings?*

WB: This is an interesting chair. I had a call from Bill Hammond, who sells our furniture in Dallas. He was then working on the Johnson Library, and he said that the president [Lyndon Johnson] really would like an all-wood chair. Amusingly enough, he said he'd like it sort of between a barroom chair and a courtroom chair, with a little bit of a western saddle.

BLDD: *And that's what you gave him?*

WB: That's it! This happens to me constantly now. Last weekend, a firm in California called Gensler—one of our largest interior design firms—requested that I work on two pieces of furniture for a new building.

BLDD: *They also made another unusual request. Am I correct that you went out there to talk with their employees?*

WB: I spoke to two hundred employees in San Francisco. Then I gave two lectures at Berkeley, and I think half of those same employees came back for part two. I showed them slides of buildings. The lecture was basically on the idea of total design, which is my true love: to design everything, clothes, belt buckles, you name it. I showed them slides beginning with Robert Adam and then going into Charles Rennie Mackintosh. And at the same time, Louis Sullivan, Frank Lloyd Wright, Victor

20

Horta and Antonio Gaudi and then to the Viennese, to Josef Hoffmann and Otto Wagner and then Le Corbusier. I showed them the whole history of designer-architects who were designing practically everything. Then I showed them some of my own things. And I explained to them how I design a chair, about which they had no idea.

BLDD: *Tell us too, won't you?*

WB: I design a chair by starting with a chair, any chair—it can be a Bentwood chair or an eighteenth-century French chair. The only thing I'm interested in is the pitch. The back, the lower lumbar. I might cut the arms off; I might cut the legs off, and put it on a box. But I want to be able to sit in it. So I start with that pitch, which is easy to find. It's easy if you can eliminate the arms and legs. And so, starting with that pitch, I then work with muslin, a staple gun and cardboard. Say, for instance, I wanted to make a low chair into a highback chair. I would take a couple of strong photographic clips and a huge piece of cardboard, and clip it on. And then I would start drawing on the cardboard to get the shape. It's an armature. It's no different from sculpture, or even making dresses.

BLDD: *I guess that also explains your best-known chair, where the armature is literally exposed to the observer. It's in thousands of homes and offices throughout the country.*

WB: I love the skeleton showing. I really like chairs that show everything. Which is, of course, the case with a good eighteenth-century French *bergère*. Everything shows—in contrast to covering over, so you don't see anything. That can be very comfortable and very practical and very successful. But I prefer to see the bones.

BLDD: *What is the next step in the design?*

WB: After I have my pitch, I decide on the shape of the chair, and then its height, which is dictated by the length from your ankle to your knee. The height of the arm is dictated by another position. It all has to do with the human body, and it goes back to the Greeks. The Greeks made bucket seats in straw. There are marvelous copies of the Greek straw chairs, made by Bielecky. And they are exactly as the Greeks' were. If you wiggle yourself around in the sand and make a hole, you're going to make yourself a bucket. And so the height of the arm, the height of the leg, and also the height of the neck, for a top executive chair, are all dictated by the human form.

BLDD: *You are obviously a very influential teacher—you've taught at Yale, and at Pratt, and over many a dinner table. Many of your students have described your influence on them. Is there any way that they have influenced you?*

WB: You never stop learning. I was working on a new table with a draftswoman; she's a student, and she's working part-time down at the studio at Brickel. And she came up with something this week that I couldn't quite figure out. Hans Hofmann always said that he got more from his students than the students got from him. And I believe that is true. You never know where that lovely little inspiration will come out. I remember some housewives in an evening class here, a couple of years ago. I was a critic, and Michael Kalil was the teacher. I couldn't believe there was such beautiful work being done by women who had never studied before in their lives. They were doing houses, and it was thrilling. I learned a great deal from it. It's sort of give and take.

BLDD: *You've said, "I strongly disagree with and disapprove of most people who are doing interiors today." Can you elaborate on that? What is it that you disapprove of so strongly?*

WB: In California, I visited Charles Moore's Sea Ranch. We walked around and went into the condominium. And every apartment in that condominium looked as if it had been furnished at Bloomingdale's. It was shocking. There was no personality. They all had the same furniture, the same outdoor furniture, the same glasses, the same everything. You didn't know whose apartment you were in.

BLDD: *Is that better or worse than houses or apartments of forty years ago that were furnished from the attic or with flotsam and jetsam of make-do furnishings? Which do you prefer? Or is there an alternative?*

WB: I think if we go back a little further, to handcrafted furniture, such as Stickley, or say, "post office" furniture, there was something else about it.

BLDD: *But it wasn't so cherished at the time. It is only recently that we've come to assign an esthetic or a monetary value to some of that furniture.*

WB: I think those styles stayed around a while, though. After all, whatever it was, good or bad, it was there; it wasn't just around for six months, it wasn't just being in vogue. It's all fashion now. Everything is sort of clever; all of a sudden in the last five years the colors all became pastel. It was fashion, the same as the dress business.

BLDD: *Some of that fashion seems to have affected you as well; I notice you have developed a new line of textiles that has some of the most beautiful pastel colors imaginable.*

WB: Not all are pastels!

BLDD: *Some of them are . . .*

WB: Oh, well, indeed. We *are* in business. My furniture is to be sold, you know. There are pieces of furniture I like that simply do not sell—my favorites, as a matter of fact.

BLDD: *What are your favorites?*

WB: It would be hard to describe them. One, called the "envelope" chair, does not sell. The "H-frame" chair does not sell. And there's furniture that I would like to take off the line, but can't because it's selling. I have to be practical; that gives me my freedom. We work with hundreds and thousands of architects throughout the country; if certain fabrics are requested, we'll make any color any architect wants, as long as they buy a certain yardage.

BLDD: *Was there ever an order for a color you rejected because you thought it was an assault on your design?*

WB: Oh, no. And no one is allowed to change my furniture. I own the designs; Brickel manufactures them, and takes care of all the business arrangements that I'm not interested in. The only thing I'm involved in is the esthetics. I work with a firm

Ward Bennett
"Sled" chair
1962

on the advertising, on the graphics and also on the quality control.

BLDD: *You touched on a point that has interested me. I notice more and more chairs throughout the country, both in homes and in offices, that look like modest and sometimes cheap—I mean in execution, not design—versions of a Ward Bennett chair. How is that possible? How can they copy that chair? Do you have any protection for your design?*

WB: No, I own the designs in the sense that I get a royalty on the design, but it isn't patented. If Brickel stops making a chair, the design comes back to me and I could perhaps have someone else manufacture it. But the problem with rip-offs is that there are now thirteen copies made of our furniture.

BLDD: *Economically, that is not the highest form of flattery.*

WB: It is in a way. Actually, we have problems producing the furniture, there's so much business.

BLDD: *But why isn't it patented?*

WB: You can't patent designs; you can't patent a dress. The same thing happens with people copying a Dior design. You can patent a zipper, you can patent some other sort of closing, but you cannot patent a shape.

BLDD: *And what is the thinking behind that?*

WB: I don't know. Lawyers have been working on it for years.

BLDD: *Is that also the case for your flatware? You've designed flatware for Tiffany's. Is that patented?*

WB: No. Tiffany wanted to produce a design of mine in silver, and it turned out to be too expensive. I think they produced one hundred settings. Six months later, the then vice president, George O'Brien, sent me a letter with a full-page ad of my Tiffany silver, being produced in stainless steel by Supreme Cutlery. I called them, and I got no response whatsoever. I had my lawyer write them a letter, and it also got no response. Six months later, again, I wrote a letter to the president of the company, Mr. Julian Rosenberg, and I said, in effect, "If you wanted an original design, and you didn't want to knock off somebody else's, why don't you get in touch with me?

BLDD: *Did he?*

WB: These are the people who now produce my stainless steel flatware! They discontinued the first design, but I just signed a contract for another three years, for three other place settings. They simply didn't have any experience working with designers. They're perfectly nice people, but they simply didn't know how to go about it.

BLDD: *Maybe they don't know how to go about it, and it may be that, in some small way, it is the fault of the profession itself. Somehow we have failed to communicate to other people either the availability or the importance of design. Because once you suggested it to Mr. Rosenberg, he responded exactly as you would have liked him to.*

WB: It is a paradox. There are no agents for designers, as there are for writers, actors, and for many other professions. I don't understand it.

BLDD: *Is good design thought of as a precious commodity, or is it thought of as so universally attainable that you don't need someone to represent you?*

WB: It's complicated. There are very few designers, oddly enough. We're only talking about ten top firms. We just had a meeting in Los Angeles with the top designers, including Italians and Germans who had come over. And there were twenty designers there who were the so-called top designers globally.

BLDD: *You have many ties to Italy, where you've lived and worked over a long period of time. Do you think that Italy is the design capital today, as it was ten and twenty years ago?*

WB: No, I don't at all. For one thing, there's been no architecture in Italy. The economics have always been so poor there that they have done very few new buildings. So the architects there went into interior design. But in Italy right now, the furniture is beginning to look the way the Scandinavian furniture did ten years ago. Here was a whole Scandinavian boom, and for a while it looked so right. When I was working at Chase Manhattan Bank twenty years ago, we used thousands

22

Ward Bennett
Flatware and mugs
1972

of Wegner chairs. Now, the Italian designs have begun to seem very plastic, very synthetic.

BLDD: *Is there a design capital today? And if there is one, where is it?*

WB: It's right here in New York, I believe.

BLDD: *What are some of the good things being made here today? Are there a lot of beautiful things that one can buy at an affordable price?*

WB: Most of the firms in the so-called top ten in New York do not sell to department stores because their funiture is hand-made, and therefore too expensive to produce. Bloomingdale's couldn't sell it; it would cost too much. All our things are very expensive; I wish they were less so.

BLDD: *Do you have a lower-priced line, or, if you don't, any intention of developing one?*

WB: I would if I had the opportunity. I'm allowed to do a line of plastics or hospital furniture—anything that is not competitive with my present line. I'd like very much to work for a firm like Herman Miller.

BLDD: *What would you do for them if asked?*

WB: Certainly, because of their technology, I would get involved in plastics, in fiberglass. I love their hospital line; I think they also do wonderful things in residential furniture. Our furniture is basically top executive furniture. It's a very small market. It's really top exec, it's not the secretarial pool.

BLDD: *Speaking of top executives, you had about a seven-year association with the Lehigh Furniture Company. During that time, you were asked to design a special chair for a very top executive, one David Rockefeller. What were the circumstances of that design, and what was his request?*

WB: I was hired when One Chase Manhattan Plaza was built nineteen years ago, as David Rockefeller's consultant, working with Skidmore, Owings & Merrill. I was employed by David Rockefeller. So there were literally thousands of pieces of my furniture used in that building. But I did design a particular desk chair for David Rockefeller. It has a very good lumbar support. He had a difficult back—from a ski accident, I think. So the chair had a good high back where he could rest his head, and it had a very good lower lumbar support. It also had some mechanical movement.

BLDD: *Do you use medical research in designing a chair to determine what is the most comfortable position and the most therapeutic?*

WB: Indeed. I had a back problem and still do. I had worked for a long time for [John F.] Kennedy's doctor, Dr. Janet Travell, when my back really first went out. And it was through working with her that I developed my first chair. There wasn't a chair on the market that she considered comfortable, other than the rocking chair she prescribed for President Kennedy.

BLDD: *You're among the first designers to employ industrial materials in residential design. Why did you begin to do that?*

WB: Because they're so beautiful. I think Le Corbusier once described the best American architecture as being the silos and the industrial buildings and the dams. I like anything that's made like a camera—they way it moves, the connections, the strength are innately beautiful.

BLDD: *One of the most widely illustrated of your interiors is your own apartment. It is in a gable in the landmark Dakota on the West Side of Manhattan. It was once a warren of servants' rooms and it is surely one of the most striking interiors, with the most magnificent view of New York and Central Park that exists. You took that space and scooped it out when the building first became a cooperative in the 1960s. Recently, you redesigned it. Why did you want a third incarnation for that space, and how did it evolve?*

WB: It's my profession, you know! As I develop new things, I always bring new designs to the house, or to the studio on the eighth floor, to live with them and try them. The apartment is really a workshop, even though I live there. I'm bringing a new chair that I'm fond of up this week; I can't wait to get it home. One of the reasons is that I want to see it in an environment that's not just drafting tables or the factory. I want

23

Ward Bennett
"Metro" flatware
1977

to see how it relates to other pieces of furniture.

BLDD: *It seems to me that as your style has evolved it has become a tiny bit more luxurious, even softer. Is this new design a search for physical comfort, or something deeper?*

WB: All my designs are related to comfort, always. If it's not comfortable, than I certainly would discard it. It must really be comfortable. That is a requirement. I learned a lot about that from a friend who is in a wheelchair, having visited her for a long time in a polio ward, how necessary it is to support the bottom of your feet. That's one of the many theories I have about comfort and how to keep your back in a chair. I always use a couple of telephone books myself.

BLDD: *I suspect that not all designers share your view about comfort being the primary criterion for design. I wonder if this is an era where anything goes—is there still a rigid standard of what's in and what's out? And what is?*

WB: That depends, again, on the place. If you live in Japan—and that's changing very much now—you have grown up sitting on the floor, and your bones and muscles have formed to be able to do so. I can't do that. And in India they can squat for hours. If you're living in our society you are either working in an office or are eating or writing in your home; the comfort of what you're sitting in is different. I think the chair is the most important design since squatting for daily living. There are two other horizontal surfaces, the bed and the table. So I think with the bed and the table and the chair, that's it. I'll always remember Fra Angelico's little cell in Florence, where he did his fantastic paintings. There was a table and a bed and a chair. That's all you need.

BLDD: *Are there regional differences in taste? Is the West Coast more experimental and the East more sophisticated?*

WB: Yes, I think so. Certainly I think the East is more sophisticated.

BLDD: *What do you consider good taste?*

WB: I hate the word.

24 BLDD: *What word would you substitute?*

WB: I don't like the words "good taste." I almost prefer the words "bad taste." Good taste is dictated by the Diana Vreelands in life. You have to wear this, you have to wear that. You're short and fat, but you have to wear Calvin Klein clothes that don't suit you. This business of taste is something to question. I think people should develop their own taste, through education, by really working on it. They should study and go to museums, not just for something to do, like going to the movies—but really to understand our heritage. They should make certain that whatever they have is truly meaningful to them, that it isn't just some bric-a-brac. Most homes are full of meaningless things. Most houses you go to you will not remember as you would remember another type of interior—a restaurant in Paris, for instance. They're just splendid, and not necessarily done by a decorator.

BLDD: *It's been more than fifty years since you overturned that hand truck on the corner of Thirty-third Street. And everything you've explored appears to have been not only a great success for you, but gratifying, as well. How has success influenced the way you live and work—has it created any barriers or problems, or has it simplified or facilitated things for you?*

WB: My life is very simple. I have everything I want materially, and I want very little. I love to travel. Georgia O'Keeffe made a statement to me recently. Happily, I had four hours with her—a fantastic lady, almost blind and eighty-nine or something. We had many friends in common in the past. In leaving, she said to me, "You know, Ward, there's only one thing that matters. Only one. Is it interesting?"

Ward Bennett
"University" carved-wood frame
armchair
1980

Following pages:
Ward Bennett's study/bedroom
1970

Ward Bennett
Round carved-wood frame
armchair
1967

Ward Bennett seated on
"Alexandria" chair
1975

Ward Bennett's living room
1970

BLDD: *Design partners since 1970, Bob Bray and Mike Schaible have handled everything from a one-room apartment to a 100,000-square-foot building. In theory, Bray specializes in creative design while Schaible runs the business. Why don't you tell us how it works in practice?*

BB: I think we're still trying to find out exactly how we do it. We've had some real problems in ten years of business. It has been extremely difficult at times. Now, Mike is probably my best friend; I call him family at this point. But we've had some rough moments. Basically, we're two very strong egos, and he really did think that it was his business. And I really did think it was my business. Now we think it's *our* business.

BLDD: *What does it take to make a partnership work, let alone work well? Perhaps you can tell us, Mike?*

MS: Just working very closely together—argue a lot, agree a lot.

BLDD: *Why don't we get down to the way the collaboration actually operates. How do you approach a job? Who does what?*

BB: It varies in every instance, really. I usually start the design. Mike comes over and says, "I hate it," and then we sit down and work on it together.

BLDD: *What's step two? Which of you does the renderings, makes the selection of furniture, lighting and so on?*

MS: Bob does all the sketches and all the renderings. We pretty much just select everything else—either together or he selects it and I say yes or no.

BLDD: *Does either of you have the right to veto?*

MS: We both do.

BLDD: *Who has the last word in the end?*

BB: We simply have never had that problem.

BLDD: *Do you ever use each other as a buffer zone between the firm and the client?*

MS: Oh, sure.

BLDD: *I can imagine Mrs. Jones on the telephone. There she is for the fourth time, because the carpenter has yet to show up, and neither of you wants to get on the telephone. I understand your position, but whom does she turn to for relief?*

MS: It depends what's happening and who's been dealing with that part of the project. Sometimes I refer her to Bob. Or he refers her back to me, and by that time she's cooled down.

BLDD: *Are you both equally involved in all the jobs that you do?*

BB: Totally.

BLDD: *You both have strong convictions and a very firm point of view. How do you manage to subsume either a design point of view, or your ego, at any given point?*

BB: They seem to coincide. I'm not sure how that came about. But it really is not much of a problem.

BLDD: *Why don't we backtrack for a moment and find out how this all began. What path led each of you to interior design? Did you major in design as students?*

BB: I started much earlier than that—at six years old, going home and shoving the furniture around the apartment. And all my father would hear at two or three o'clock in the morning was crash, bam . . .

BLDD: *So you became very careful about where you placed furniture. What was life like when you lived in very small towns? I know that Bob comes from Oklahoma and Mike from Colorado. Why don't we start with you, Mike?*

MS: It's a town of 1,800 people called Akron, Colorado. I couldn't wait to get out.

BB: His mother was the mayor.

MS: The biggest influence on me at the time was my mother. We'd go home and move the appliances from one side of the kitchen to the other. We spent a lot of time doing that. I was real anxious to get away from home.

BLDD: *Was being mayor a full-time occupation?*

MS: Oh no, she was also a florist.

BLDD: *Did you work in the flower shop?*

MS: Not too much. Then I went to the University of Colorado and studied interior design. The head of the department had

Bray & Schaible

graduated from Parsons, so I came to Parsons. I loved the university and I loved Parsons. It was a great way to get away from home.

BLDD: *Where did the two of you meet?*

BB: We met at Parsons.

BLDD: *You also came from a very small town, Bob, Fox, Oklahoma. What's the population of Fox?*

BB: I'm not sure, but I didn't live in town, I lived outside of town.

BLDD: *Did you live on a farm?*

BB: No, we lived in the middle of the oil fields. There were some farms but I didn't live on one.

BLDD: *Was there a particular person or a circumstance there that most influenced you?*

BB: I idolized my brother. He was eight years older, and had a major influence on my work; he led me to design actually. He had written a letter to Albert Camus, and he had gotten a response. I thought that was terrific, so I wrote one to Frank Lloyd Wright.

BLDD: *Did you get a response?*

BB: I certainly did. I received several letters.

BLDD: *What did you ask him?*

BB: I don't remember what I asked in the first letter. But I remember going down to the mailbox and pulling out that parchment envelope with a big FLW seal stamped on it—I was just in heaven. The first two letters were actually from Frank Lloyd Wright himself. Those were wonderful times.

BLDD: *Did that influence your choice of a career? You studied architectural engineering, I believe.*

BB: I did.

BLDD: *With a plan to doing what?*

BB: I was always interested in interiors, but the schools were not very good. They were not good at all. So I studied architectural engineering, and then came to Parsons. At Parsons I met Alan Tate. I was very impressed to see a man doing what I wanted to do—against great odds, standing up against a lot of pressure. He reorganized the school, simply did what he had to do. And with no help.

BLDD: *He recently paid the two of you the ultimate compliment: he asked you to design his apartment. Why did he need, or want, an interior designer?*

MS: He felt that he had been in every position—teacher, designer, student. He had done everything except be a client. So he decided he would be a client. He liked our work and asked us to do his apartment.

BLDD: *What did you do for him?*

MS: First of all, the project scared us to death. We thought, "What the hell does he want from us?" Then we started talking and it became very exciting, because of his way of living, his collections, his artwork. It was really very exciting and interesting. I think he was nervous in the beginning too—as nervous as we were, though you wouldn't expect it.

BLDD: *What did you design for him?*

BB: We did a couple of complicated things that we would not normally do for a typical client. It's a furniture plan that under normal circumstances doesn't work. A special person living there makes it work.

BLDD: *Can you describe the design?*

BB: There's a banquette, about nine feet long, with only one way to get in, which you wouldn't do ordinarily. There's a table in front of the banquette that is anchored to the floor. I'd known him for many years, and every time I had visited he was always somehow working at some table. There'd be a piece of art that he was working on, or a typewriter, drawing, or letters. It was that little bit of information that led to the design.

BLDD: *Why don't we talk about another specific assignment? One of your larger assignments, and a recent one as well, was the restructuring and design of a two-story maisonette in a grand old Park Avenue building that included, in addition to a standard living room, dining room, kitchen, bath and bedrooms, a library, bar, playroom and maid's room. In redesign-* 33

ing and redefining the space, it appears that you set out to design not only rooms, but rooms within rooms. What was your intention?

BB: You just hit it; rooms within rooms. People talk about getting these great spaces and wanting to move into a really large apartment. We've seen this many times. Then when they get it, they stay in the little back room, the little library, or the sitting room off the bedroom, and the large spaces are untouched.

BLDD: *Are they too intimidating?*

BB: They are intimidating. When you are home alone, or even with one other person, rooms that are thirty by seventy feet are just not comfortable. We tried to create a shell within a shell.

BLDD: *What made you decide to retain some of the older elements, or choose other elements to introduce into the scheme?*

MS: Any time there's something really beautiful, we'll work with it. If it's ugly, or doesn't work, we'll try to remove it. Many moldings were beautiful. Many of the shapes were beautiful. We couldn't touch the windows; they were a special height, so that was a given. The library was very special; the paneling is beautiful. So we kept that.

BLDD: *I think of you fellows as being very genial and responsive to your clients' needs—but actually, somewhere you once said, "We ask them directly what they like and dislike, but we take the dislikes with a grain of salt." Were you kidding then—or if not, why do you ask them?*

BB: We were not kidding at all. It happens so many times that someone will tell you he absolutely hates purple. Then he will show you something he wants you to see because he really likes it. You go look at it, and say, "Yes, but this is purple."

BLDD: *So, many times someone's stated dislikes mean nothing...*

MS: We realize that from our own life, our own homes, and in designs. I say I hate something, and then all of a sudden I pick up a picture and there it is, and I know I don't hate it.

BLDD: *How do you live? What sort of environments have you created for yourselves?*

BB: I've spent the last two months doing small scribblings on all the walls in my one-room studio. I don't own a chair now. I took the last chair out of there. I have two folding chairs, but I rarely use those. I am not your normal apartment dweller. When I go home, I pace a lot. I'm continually plotting and thinking about what I'm going to do with my career or with a particular project that I'm working on. I write on sketch pads or the nearest wall. The entire apartment gets messy, but I'm a fanatic about cleanliness. Things may pile up, but as long as I can also do work, it's fine.

BLDD: *Did you always live that way, or did you decide to pare down your environment to its most minimal?*

BB: I've lived in every scale of apartment. I had one apartment that was about 4,000 square feet, and I lived in a twelve-foot-square area. It was ridiculous for me to maintain all that. Most of my interest was outside the apartment and still is.

BLDD: *Do you live in such a spare way, as well, Mike?*

MS: It's spare, but I have a bigger apartment and I have things. Not a lot, it's very organized. I can't stand piles all over.

BB: We don't visit each other often.

MS: I haven't been in Bob's apartment in two or three years.

BLDD: *How much, minimally, does a Bray-Schaible job cost these days, and what's the lowest-priced job you'll take on?*

MS: The lowest job that we can work on right now is $50,000 for the total budget, but we haven't taken jobs at that cost in a while. Fortunately, our business has grown and we've been able to do this. We're now working on a job that's $1 million.

BLDD: *What does a client get for $1 million?*

MS: *Everything*, including a couple of designers who are under their feet from the crack of dawn!

BLDD: *They deserve everything at those rates! Where does the money go, specifically, in a million-dollar job?*

MS: To the client who can spend $1 million, it means the same

34

Michael Schaible's bedroom
1979

thing as the client who can spend $10,000. Someone who could spend $10,000 may sit down and think, "God, if I had a million, what could I do?" But it's not the same thing—clients with a million dollars to spend have bigger apartments. You may be able to tear out every wall, you may be able to have skylights, greenhouses, complete new bathrooms and kitchens.

BLDD: *How much did the Park Avenue apartment that you redefined and restructured cost?*

BB: I'm not sure what that was. It was not a big budget.

BLDD: *It looks like an enormous renovation.*

BB: It wasn't. I think it was $250,000 or $300,000.

BLDD: *$250,000 or $300,000 sounds like a* very *big budget. How was that money spent?*

BB: I can give that to you very quickly. We get totally involved in the architecture. If you have a triplex with a hundred windows, and the client wants new windows, that's $150,000 right there. The same amount would be spent just on wall air conditioning or heating units. So far we've done nothing to make our eight-by-ten glossies look good. But we've spent a lot of money just on the mechanics of an apartment. A kitchen these days—a good kitchen—costs about $50,000 to $75,000 and it's easy for it to be $150,000.

BLDD: *Is that true only in New York, and only for a very ritzy kitchen?*

BB: If you call an excellent contractor and have him come in and put new fixtures on all your bathroom fittings and re-tile your bathroom, it will be $10,000 at least. And that's not moving anything.

BLDD: *But I don't understand why a kitchen costs $50,000. It seems to me that a refrigerator costs several thousand dollars, and the best stove must cost the same thing. Even with the addition of air vents and cabinets, how can it all add up to so much?*

MS: Again, you have to go back to the architecture. Many times in old buildings the plumbing is gone, the electricity is gone. So you have to install all new electricity and plumbing.

BLDD: *A lot of the costs, then, are really hidden costs. And as yet, we really haven't talked about the role of an interior designer. Incidentally, do you call yourselves interior designers? Are you decorators, are you space planners?*

BB: All of the above. We're not fussy about the title.

MS: I would say we refer to ourselves as interior designers. But we are all of them.

BLDD: *What's the difference between an interior designer and a decorator?*

MS: Some jobs we go in and start working on the architecture, tearing it apart, working on the electricity and the plumbing, really working with the structure. Then, sometimes we do a decorating job where we apply things and move in funiture, but don't really get involved in the structure.

BB: The processes are never defined very well. They overlap: decorators do design work, designers do the work of a decorator.

BLDD: *What about the role of the architect—how does that come into this?*

BB: I don't know where they are! Back to my point about design and decoration. If you need a dining chair in your dining room, you can go out and do wonderful selective buying and purchase something. To me, that's decoration. If you can't find what you need, you can design the chair. That's design.

BLDD: *In that Park Avenue apartment, you not only designed the space, you also decorated it. But you modified the color scheme which we usually identify with you—gray, and black and white—to include some softer tones, including a very luscious vanilla and pink and taupe. In fact, it's a very mellow version of your usual palette. Why did you choose to do that? Is that a change in the direction of your design and your approach?*

MS: I think it's many things. In the beginning, with the budget you try to spend the money the best way possible. And if it's a low budget, you think of maintenance. The dark black and charcoal grays really had a lot to do with that. It was the best carpet for the money. It held up the best; it was the best to maintain. When you have a larger budget, you can start going into some other materials. But for some of the low-budget jobs that we did in the beginning, we picked the best materials we knew.

BLDD: *Would you still advocate them for a low-budget job?*
MS: Sure.
BLDD: *Do you ever use them in your more expensive work as well?*
BB: We do.
MS: It depends. It has so much to do with so many things. It is design, but it's also function, and people want a place that will be easy to maintain, no matter what the budget is.
BB: I don't think anyone really knows how the high-tech and minimalism thing came about for many of the best designers. We were very traditionally trained. I love antiques. We know a lot about antiques and about period design. We went to Parsons in the days when once a week, in the Metropolitan Museum, you would sit on a little folding stool all day long and trace the shell motif of a very good Queen Anne chair. And you learned to love those things. When we started working, we were making things out of nothing. Someone would come to us with $9,000 to do a two-bedroom apartment. Yet we had been trained to love quality, so of course, we could not touch a reproduction. We just simply wouldn't. And the high-tech components were a whole body of untapped materials. Yet, they were real, each item was real. They were good.
BLDD: *Do you still use them now that you're in the high-budget area?*
BB: Absolutely.
BLDD: *What, for example, are some of your favorite Bray-Schaibleisms of high tech?*
BB: That's not the way it comes about. It's when you're working on a particular plan, and you think, yes, that would solve this problem very well.
BLDD: *So it's a specific solution to a specific problem. But*

there must be some devices or design effects that you particularly like, either in hardware or furnishings—for example, the gray carpeting.
MS: There was one thing that we used a lot of in a flower shop that we did: it was one of our first jobs, at the General Motors Building, for Terrestris. The ceiling was all hung in steel subway grating. We've continued to use steel grating over the years, and I guess we did become known for using it. Other designers were using it too. Then we were contacted by Bloomingdale's wanting to know if we would be interested in doing a line of subway grating furniture. So all of a sudden it was taken completely out of the context of what we were doing.
BLDD: *Were you interested in doing a line of subway grating furniture?*
MS: We laughed.
BLDD: *Can we expect to see the use of more antique furniture and objects in your environments in the future?*
MS: You may.
BLDD: *Would you like to do an interior with antiques?*
BB: Always did.
BLDD: *Have you done any?*
BB: We've never had the opportunity. Well, a few—maybe four spaces that have really wonderful things.
BLDD: *You said before you would not use reproductions. A number of designers whom we've talked to felt that it was rather limiting not to use reproductions, if the reproductions are of quality. In a world of diminishing resources—particularly money, let alone the objects themselves—they felt that it was not only acceptable, it was even desirable from time to time to use first-rate reproductions. Do you agree?*
BB: I don't feel as strongly about it now, but I would like to see alternatives. I would like to see something more inventive.
BLDD: *I know that you work closely with clients throughout the planning and execution of a project. Do you ever require or urge that they get rid of the furnishings that they've had before you start the job?*

MS: Yes, and no. Sometimes we say, "If we're going to do this job, we can't deal with this furniture." It is true that there's no way we can work with ugly furniture that has nothing to do with what our spaces are like.

BLDD: *How do clients come to you in the first place? From time to time, clients make a mistake, as do designers in selecting which clients they will work with—I assume that sometimes happens. But since your work is known for a particular look, they must be aware of the kind of environment you're going to create for them.*

MS: They've either been to a space, or they've seen our publicity. Even at that point, we ask them to come to our office for the first meeting. We show them our portfolio and talk about what we do. We do not talk about their job at all. We just talk about what we've done and what we're about and how we work. If they're interested, the next step is to go to their apartment and to see it and see what they're about, specifically. This is very important, and a lot of people don't realize that. They think it only matters if they are interested in us. But it's a two-way street, and a long, long road.

BLDD: *How long does the average job take nowadays?*

MS: About a year. Clients have to plan on a year of upheaval—and I guess a lot more than that.

BLDD: *We've already become accustomed to your sense of whimsy. A card you've written to your clients goes something like, "When you care enough to spend every cent you have..." How do people react to that?*

BB: This came about when some friends were starting a new newspaper and wanted us to take a page for an ad. We don't do advertising. But I liked them, so I wanted to do something humorous.

BLDD: *What did the ad say?*

BB: Exactly that: "When you care enough to spend every cent you have." And then at the bottom it said "Bray-Schaible."

BLDD: *Have you gotten any clients as a result of the ad?*

MS: Yes. They're wonderful. After the newspaper came out, we sent it to many of our clients. We didn't hear from a couple of them so I called and said, "What did you think?" They didn't find it amusing at all. And I felt it told a lot about *them.* Most clients loved it, and would show it to their friends as if it were a postcard.

BLDD: *How close to the original amount that you've budgeted does a job end up costing?*

MS: We used to do preliminary budgets, and say the job would come in around ten percent over our estimate. It did; how, we don't know.

BB: For about the first eight years, Mike did very tight budgets and all of our projects came in within three percent.

MS: There are just a few people who can make that.

BLDD: *Is that one of the hallmarks of success?*

BB: It's an incredible amount of work. And it's harder to work now than it was.

MS: We try to get an indication of the budget from clients. We hope that they have some idea. And then we put it in the back of our mind, and proceed to do exactly what we're going to do, with the understanding with the clients that the budget may be over, but they're in full control. We know ways we can cut, but it doesn't happen often, because the clients usually want what they see.

BLDD: *You said it's much harder to work now. I guess anybody who's ever tried to have a faucet repaired has some idea of what life must be like for you on a daily basis. What is the most urgent problem, the greatest grievance you have in your work these days? Is it the unavailability of craftspeople? Is it a lack of quality, is it the inability to deliver things, or that once they have been delivered they don't come in the right color, or in one piece?*

MS: All of those things.

BB: I think there still are a lot of craftspeople in this city. Most of the problems stem from time. A contractor will swear he can do a one-year job in three months.

BLDD: *But you know better?*

Robert Bray and Michael Schaible
First National Bank of Hialeah
Hialeah, Florida
1976

MS: You can't convince clients. Some clients won't listen. Six months later they will.

BB: An incredible number of problems stem from that.

BLDD: *Have you ever fired a client?*

BB: Yes.

BLDD: *On what basis?*

BB: Ignorance.

BLDD: *And how is that demonstrated?*

MS: We weren't getting any place and they weren't getting any place. It just didn't work.

BB: It was a project we had broken into two separate contracts, for the architecture and for the interior.

BLDD: *So you finished phase one but didn't go to the interior?*

BB: Yes, we wouldn't touch the next one.

BLDD: *You once had a very unusual commission, from* Playboy *magazine—to create a fantasy penthouse. That's hardly a typical assignment. How did it come about?*

BB: We took that money and went into business. That was about ten years ago. On a two-week vacation from another design office where we were working, we chugged things out every night and did eight pages of illustrations and plans.

BLDD: *What was the fantasy penthouse like?*

BB: This particular one was quite vulgar. And because we had to turn it out quickly, you'll notice most of those spaces are painted right off the same palette.

BLDD: *What would you do now if you had the same assignment?*

MS: Turn it down.

BB: We probably wouldn't be interested in that assignment. Pepsi-Cola of Arabia wanted that apartment. We got an incredible letter—his credentials across the top, all the ice, all the dairy products, Pepsi-Cola. And at the end it said, "Playboy Club Key Holder." These were his credentials.

MS: We got many letters and calls from people like that—*real* playboys who had to have this pad. It was just disgusting.

BB: We'd really arrived.

BLDD: *What's your idea of an ideal client? Should they be involved with what you do, or say, "Here's our space, here's our budget. We know what you're about, you have some idea of our interest, and we'll give you a little list of particulars. Please, we want to come back and move into this apartment." I guess that's the fantasy of anybody who's ever lived through a paint job.*

MS: No, the ideal client is one whom you really become involved with in the project. There's a great deal of input from the client.

BLDD: *You have very firm points of view. And however gentle the touch is, I don't know how easy it would be for a client to be as persuasive as he or she would like to be with the two of you. How do they get an opportunity to be part of the design process?*

MS: It just happens. We start talking. They may say something like, "I don't think that works. I'm not sure about that." And my immediate reaction is, "Well, then go to hell." But I have to keep cool. Bob's thinking, and then I start thinking, and I think, "They're right." Many times it ends up better because of this input.

BB: Most of the complaints you get are valid. The client's solution is usually terrible, but the complaint is valid.

BLDD: *They know there's something wrong with it, and it's up to you to resolve it in a more esthetically pleasing way. But you don't do much shopping with your clients. Your notion is really to create a design and to present material. Is that accurate?*

MS: Yes. We will go out for specific items, a chair, for example, and take the client to see that particular chair. We don't take clients out to see all chairs.

BB: We do shop, but when we're shopping we're looking for something special, unique, it's a major project. This may require letters all over the world. You have to search for something specific.

BLDD: *What have you done that required letters all over the world?*

BB: In New Orleans I just saw, totally by accident, an extraordinary William and Mary double bonnet highboy. I got on the telephone immediately trying to track that down, and it had just been moved. We don't do a lot of this.

BLDD: *Did you find it?*

MS: It was sold.

BB: No way to get it back.

BLDD: *Where were you going to use it?*

BB: On a project here.

BLDD: *What does the rest of the room look like?*

BB: It has wood floors with planks about ten inches wide that are separated like an old tassel floor. Very high ceilings, Kasota stone chimney pieces. We moved several tons of Kasota stone into that dining room.

BLDD: *Is Kasota stone the same pinkish colored stone that you used for the Park Avenue apartment dining table? Where is it from?*

MS: Minnesota.

BLDD: *How did you discover it?*

BB: We have boxes of materials that are sent to us. It was just one of those that I've always liked.

BLDD: *You do not often place furniture against walls. You do however, lean paintings against walls. Why do you prefer that to hanging them?*

BB: It's not really a preference. It's just an alternative that I like. It usually happens because someone says, "I like what you did there, can I do that here?" You simply say "Yes." It's not a big issue. The first time we actually did this was for Paul Harper, who had an incredible collection of paintings and drawings. There was no way they could all be put up even if they were floor to ceiling in every room in the house. We took one room and made bins for all his art, and he rotated the works on a regular basis. It's a wonderful experience. They look at them more often this way, I think, by participating with them and changing them and pulling them out.

MS: We created a whole storeroom for art. The bins were just storage bins that the paintings slid into; then to display them you stand them on a ledge and lean them against the wall.

BLDD: *What happens when a client neither has a terrific collection of paintings, nor lives in a room that has floors like a castle—and, like many people, particularly in urban centers, lives by choice, or necessity, in a boxlike building with uninesting spaces? What do you do then?*

MS: We have many examples of that right here in New York in apartment buildings. They have low ceilings, ugly windows, very small boxy rooms.

BLDD: *How do you resolve the uninteresting space then?*

MS: It's really working with the architecture, moving walls or changing the shape or trying to play up the window or the view.

BB: Working in these buildings is a struggle. You want to give it any kind of uniqueness. But oddly enough, if you really labor over that plan and keep looking at it, you *can* find relationships. And if you get a glimpse of an idea, it's amazing what can come out of those simple things.

BLDD: *What job has been most satisfying to the both of you?*

MS: I think one is the Park Avenue apartment.

BLDD: *Was it because of the scale, the end result?*

MS: It was the scale, it was the client, it's doing something that you really like and having it work. It's built the way you want it. And you're pleased with how it's built. The clients are pleased, you end up friends.

BLDD: *You've done that with many of your clients, haven't you?*

BB: We have been fortunate in that respect. It's unbelievable. We have great clients. When I get together with other designers and sit around for an evening and listen to the conversations, I feel that we're practically in another business. We don't take clients for granted. We have wonderful clients and lots of them, and have had for years.

BLDD: *Another unusual compliment paid to you is that one of*

39

Robert Bray and Michael Schaible
Living room
1973

your current clients is one of the preeminent artists of our day. What are you doing for Jasper Johns?
BB: Three perfect shacks, if it kills us all, and it may.
BLDD: *What do you mean by three perfect shacks?*
MS: We're doing a house for Jasper in the Caribbean island of St. Maarten—a house, guest house and pool.
BB: He originally went to Philip Johnson. Philip had done a sketch on a napkin in 1974 and Jasper liked it and wanted us to work on the interiors, which is amazing, because it is not typical of Jasper. He does everything himself. So we went to see Philip and Philip said, "You know, Jasper professes to hate architecture, and the two of you never hang a painting on the wall." He said, "It hardly makes any sense, does it?" Then we went down to look at the property, and I called Philip and said, "Everything has changed. The house, the vista should be in another direction, the island is growing. The beautiful little house that everyone was talking about before now looks at a hill that has been bulldozed and has three hideous houses on it." So we showed him our ideas for a small house. Of course, he's entirely too busy to deal with that kind of project, really, so he said, "You should do this house." And I said, "Great, we will do this house." I've known Jasper for a while, also. So he agreed. And he said, "I don't care what you do, as long as you don't do anything I don't like."
BLDD: *What's he getting?*
BB: Three perfect shacks.
BLDD: *How do you design a building in a sunny, warm climate for someone whose works of art are sensitive to light and heat conditions—obviously that will affect what you design.*
MS: The only area there we have to worry about will be his studio. I'm sure he will not hang his work in the house. He's not known to do that.
BLDD: *What is the exterior?*
BB: It's a plain stucco house with tile roofs and tile floors of a handmade, Mexican, dried-in-the-sun tile. It's a beautiful

dusty pink with an occasional chicken or dog footprint.
BLDD: *Made while the tile was drying in the sun?*
BB: While it was drying. We meet a lot of very famous and important people. And many times, you're disappointed in the character or the aura of a person. Jasper is exceptional. The first time I met him was at his little house in Stoney Point, N.Y. Everyone was out on the terraces. The back is covered with barn doors that all open. When they're open you're up in the treetops. And there is a deck out in these treetops. Jasper was cooking five different types of mushroom that he had collected himself, cooking them five different ways. He was talking to Merce Cunningham and Louise Nevelson about design. And he was giving John Cage a haircut and beard trim. And I thought, "The Salon is still going. And I like what I see and I'm glad I'm invited, and I hope I fit." I worked very hard at it.
BLDD: *Is a job ever finished?*
BB: Well, it may or may not be.
BLDD: *How do you know if a job is finished?*
BB: They quit calling.
MS: No, they don't.

Robert Bray and Michael Schaible
Study/bedroom
1978

Robert Bray's living room
1979

Michael Schaible's living room
1979

44

Robert Bray and Michael Schaible
Dining room
1979

Robert Bray and Michael Schaible
Living room
1979

Following page:
Robert Bray and Michael Schaible
Apartment with Kasota stone
floors
1981

BLDD: *Mario Buatta provides a maximum of comfort in his exuberantly colored interiors, resulting in an unmistakable style that he calls "the undecorated look." Are you an interior designer or interior decorator or space planner? What's the difference, and how do you identify yourself?*

MB: I'm all of those things, but I like to think of myself as just an old-fashioned decorator, because I was weaned by the Syrie Maughams and the Elsie de Wolfes and the other people of that time. When I went to school back in the '50s, they were the people whom we knew about. Interior design was not much thought of in those days. We talked about design and design classes, but we thought more about decorating. Today there's a great emphasis on design.

BLDD: *How do you distinguish between the two? Isn't decoration design as well?*

MB: It is, but decoration is a somewhat old-fashioned term. I think today a lot of decorating or design students have learned a great deal more about coping with the interior structures of buildings than about decorating them. In the old days when buildings were built, architects put in all of the embellishments; there were moldings, fancy windows, even pediments over the doors, columns, pilasters, and whatever else. Today, when one gets an apartment or buys a house, it is devoid of any embellishments. There is no molding, there's barely a fireplace. You might find a mantel, if you're lucky. So one has to start from scratch. And although I do all of those things, I still think of myself as just an old-fashioned decorator.

BLDD: *Is that why you've said that even decorators need decorators?*

MB: Oh, no, I said that because even a designer or a decorator needs someone to help. We all need another pair of eyes, or someone else to come in and sort of edit what we're thinking about or what we're doing. Another decorator can inspire you to do something that you haven't thought of or can give you another point of view just by looking at what you've done or how you've treated something. It's sort of nice to hear the way they might have done it. Quite often, you've worked on a house for a very long time and you go stale. Suddenly you think, well, what am I going to do next? Maybe you've got to go away for a little while, and come back.

BLDD: *You live and work in a very fine, federal Georgian-style house, on Manhattan's Upper East Side. The walls of your library office are filled with Victorian paintings of dogs, lots of dogs, and a collection of vegetables and fruits and various forms in porcelain. How did you come to be so interested in animals, and in vegetables?*

MB: A lot of that has to do with being a human being—wanting the feeling of living in the country and yet living in the city. I was brought up in a very contemporary house. My parents built it in the '30s and furnished it with glass and steel and chrome, all the sorts of things that are terribly popular today. Many of those interiors are still left in New York and around the country, but they've been embellished over the years and grown with the people who lived in them. A lot of people who lived that way in the past are now going backwards to a more romantic idea about how they want to live. You find that a lot of people who were brought up with chrome and steel are suddenly living in very embellished kinds of rooms.

BLDD: *As you point out, we've all been influenced by our surroundings. You were raised on Staten Island surrounded by chrome and steel. How did you live? What was life like there that brought your work to such a romantic, embellished, and very English appearance?*

MB: My parents had all modern things and my mother hated anything old unless it belonged to our family. They liked to think modern and to live modern. But my mother's sister had a house that was something of an English country house and it was filled with what I used to call Thomas Chickendale furniture, and what I used to call Chinoiserie. I was just crazy about all of these things. My uncle was an architect, and I was

48

Mario Buatta

very much interested in architecture and influenced by what he was doing at the time, which was much more traditional than contemporary. So I found myself spending a great deal of time at my aunt's house. She was always decorating.

BLDD: *I've seen references to your aunt and her house, and read that every room in her house was decorated in a different period. That is an unusual point of view for a professional decorator, but it's also one to which you occasionally subscribe.*

MB: I'm not saying that my aunt's house was the greatest house ever decorated. As a matter of fact, now that I look back, a lot of mistakes were made there. She went through "periods," as people did in the '40s and '50s. They liked to change merely for the sake of changing. Much of it had to do with travel, I think. In the old days, people traveled to China and when they came back they'd add a Chinese room to their house.

BLDD: *But very few people traveled then compared with today, when many of us have the opportunity. Is that same international view reflected in the way we live now?*

MB: I think it is, but in a lesser sense. In the old days you traveled much less, it took you longer to get there, you spent more time there and a lot of time getting back, and you wanted to cherish what you'd seen. So you'd see a lot of people reproducing rooms or houses that they'd seen in their travels. Today it's so easy to get on a plane and go to London that people don't think about it very much. I think they're *too* mobile.

BLDD: *You've said that every room should tell a story. If we were to look at your library and office, what would that room tell us about you?*

MB: I feel that it's terribly important that if you come and visit me and I leave the room for a minute to get you a drink or whatever, you can look around and see that my presence is still in the room, because it's telling a story about the way I am.

BLDD: *Why don't we be specific about your room? You have a beautiful red lacquer secretary filled with botanical pot-*

tery—*how did that come about? It certainly wasn't an instant collection. . . .*

MB: No, it's taken about twenty years. It's taken all my life, actually: I started collecting when I was twelve years old. My first real find was a Sheraton writing box which I knew nothing about. It cost twelve dollars. I saved up my allowance and I paid two dollars a week for it; that's a kind of romance in itself. On my first trip to Europe as a student with the Parsons School of Design, I visited one of those great English houses and realized exactly what I'd been missing. What I love about the English is that they travel a great deal and bring things back, so a lot of their rooms tell stories. Just think about an English house: it has been lived in by seven or eight generations, added to each time, by each one, becoming more and more embellished. Each generation says, "We can't touch Aunt Catherine's collection. We've got to leave it here." So things become more and more decorated and added on to.

BLDD: *What if they're not good designs—if they just represent nostalgia?*

MB: I don't think that really matters. I think it's more important that the people living there are happy with them. What I was trying to get back to is the fact that whereas in England a family lives in one house for seven or eight generations, in America one family might move seven or eight times. So nothing is really permanent.

BLDD: *Might that not be a good thing as well, that we don't become possessed by our possessions. . . . Why don't you tell us how a young man like yourself becomes, in less than twenty years, the decorator to the rich and famous—including some very distinguished tastemakers themselves, ranging from some of the Newhouses to the president of Henri Bendel, Geraldine Stutz, and one of your current clients, Henry Ford. How did that all come about? Does one assignment lead to another?*

MB: Hard work. One assignment does lead to another. Word of mouth is usually the best publicity you can possibly have.

You can have all the pictures in the world in magazines, but people who walk into a room that you've done have to feel a certain association with that room and feel comfortable in that room.

BLDD: *Sometimes I think that it must be tough for decorators. When clients come to you, what they've seen is your last job, and I would imagine what you'd like to do is your next job. How do you bring the client along?*

MB: I really don't force myself on a client. I've decorated some pretty awful rooms in my day.

BLDD: *What, for instance, don't you want to claim anymore?*

MB: An apartment I once did for a Broadway singer; she had come to me through a very conservative client and this was my first chance to work for someone in show business. She wanted yellow walls in the living room and I thought, "Well, that's a good idea." I said, "I think the yellow will be very nice," and we painted the walls yellow. She came home that night after the show and screamed on the telephone about how I hadn't carried out her assignment. "I asked for yellow walls, a yellow room, and I want the ceilings yellow and the woodwork yellow and the windows yellow." So we painted everything yellow. The next day we papered the den, and her bedroom. It was a butterfly print with a little yellow, sort of blue and white flowers with yellow butterflies. She came home that night, and again I had a phone call. I thought, she's very delighted, she likes her paper. But she didn't like the paper at all. She said, "Where's the paper? I want the ceiling papered, I want the doors papered, and I want the furniture papered." And I said, "but you're going to lose everybody in that room." "That's the point," she said, "I don't want anybody to get out once they're in there!" It was terribly funny.

BLDD: *What are your favorite color combinations?*

MB: My favorite is yellow and blue and white.

BLDD: *Your father was a society bandleader. Have you ever thought of yourself as an entertainer?*

MB: No, not really. I think in our business we have to be part entertainer, part psychiatrist, and very much a hand-holder, helping people along.

BLDD: *Which role do you play most frequently, and which is most enjoyable?*

MB: It's interesting. Because so many people do not have a sense of humor about decorating, it becomes a very, very serious thing in their lives. After all, we're dealing with a large investment and with something they'll have to face every day. A prospective client called today. She was very serious and I started joking on the telephone, and she said, "It's *not* funny. I've just had a terrible ordeal. I'm living in an apartment that's been half-decorated by someone and it's a total mess." I couldn't help laughing and sort of trying to make her see that there was a bit of humor in it. After all, we all make mistakes. People see something you've done and they expect you to do the same thing for them. But not everybody brings out the best in you. Your jobs are only as good as your clients are.

BLDD: *You have a small office, a small staff, one assistant, one secretary, and, as contrasted to a lot of other contemporary designers or decorators, you want to keep it that way. But with that kind of limited staff, how many clients can you have each year, and how do you choose them—or do they choose you? How does it all work out? Are you going to accept this prospective client who didn't have a sense of humor, and obviously had an unsuccessful experience with someone who preceded you?*

MB: I certainly plan to see her.

BLDD: *With such a limited amount of time, why are you going to see her?*

MB: Because she sounded very nice on the telephone. She sounded as if she might need help, and if I could help her I'd be happy to. People call all the time and many aren't terribly serious about it. They're just shopping for a decorator.

BLDD: *What if this same cheerful woman lived in Rumson, New Jersey, or Cedar Rapids, Iowa?*

MB: I've got a prospective client in Rumson, New Jersey, and I

Mario Buatta's living room
18th-century French screen
Botanical porcelains
1978

keep saying I'm coming soon. . . . I will get there, eventually.

BLDD: *How can you possibly do that? There are only so many days and hours in a year. Any successful decorator such as yourself obviously has the opportunity for more clients than you can possibly manage. How do you choose?*

MB: It depends. I gauge myself, and I take only the jobs that I feel I can really be happy with. There's no point in taking on every job that comes through the door. I'm not for everybody. I'm only right for a small segment of people who understand what I'm trying to do for them. Basically I'm trying to bring their point of view out by helping them with their houses. As I said, I'm embarrassed about some of the things I've done, but the people who live in them are happy and that's what's important.

BLDD: *That's a very charitable view. How much do you learn from clients, in general?*

MB: A great deal. I've had several clients with whom the relationship has been incredible. We've helped each other, and the house just blossomed. It was like a garden that you'd worked on two or three years and then suddenly it had its most wonderful season and everything just came to life. That happens very rarely, because people don't often open up enough to accept what you're thinking and tell you what they're thinking.

BLDD: *You're a very relaxed and a very romantic fellow. What do you expect in a room? For you, what's the most important thing—the catalyst that makes a room come to life?*

MB: I think the people are. It's whom you're working with. You can pull a scheme together or pull a room together and it'll look like something that appeared in a magazine or maybe in a showroom in a department store, but the point is to work with all the different facets of one's life, to bring out all the things that you like. For example, you talk about my apartment, and you say, you've got collections of dogs, and botanical prints, and cabbages, and different forms, whether they be painted on canvas or paper, or three-dimensional. They're

things that mean a great deal to me.

Collections happen over a period of time. I bought the red lacquer bureau bookcase in England twelve years ago for a job that didn't happen to work out, and I got stuck with it and it now has a happy place. All of these things tell a story. They're all pieces that I've picked up on my travels, or that people have given me, or just things I've walked into. They become a part of you.

BLDD: *The work that you've described as ideal or pleasurable is a room or an apartment or a house that is assembled over a lifetime, and that is really autobiographical. But let's say someone comes to you without any possessions. And, let's complicate it, they also have a limited budget. They have more taste than funds—sometimes that can be challenging, too!*

MB: It can be challenging; it can also be very pleasing to work with someone like that and to work on their house over a period of time, because it does take years. I like to think of decorating a house the way an artist paints a picture—perhaps a dab at a time on the canvas until the composition comes together and it's pleasing. It's important to think about that. There's no such thing as decorating a room in six weeks or six months and saying its finished, because no room is ever finished. Rooms should be growing, living, things. I always used to say to my mother, "Is this supposed to be a *living* room? It's the deadest room in the house. You can't walk on the carpet, you can't sit on the furniture, you have to fluff the down pillows. What's the point of having this room?"

BLDD: *And how did she reply?*

MB: She let me know that this is the way their decorator had done it, and that's the way they wanted to live.

BLDD: *You want the same room, but a lived-in one?*

MB: No, I don't want the same room. I want my own room. I want what is really reflective of myself. And I try to give clients what I feel is them. There's no possible way you can give someone a background to make something look as though they've had it for many years. You can give them what some-one very jokingly called "The Instant Heritage Look."

BLDD: *Ancestor portraits?*

MB: Exactly. You can do all of those things, but if it doesn't relate to the way they go about their life every day, what is the point?

BLDD: *Your sense of color is certainly derived from your interest in art.*

MB: Yes, I think so. I remember when I was a student at the Parsons School of Design in Europe, our professor, Stanley Barrows, who was responsible for teaching a great many of the decorators whom you hear about today, took us through the Modern Museum in Paris, through the Matisse and Bonnard and Vuillard areas of the galleries. He said that if you don't understand these painters' use of color, you'll never understand the use of color, and you'll never become good decorators. It was interesting to hear that then, and it always stuck in my mind.

BLDD: *What is the key to color for you? You sometimes use bold, and unexpected combinations of colors that come off in a way that is pleasing, but surprising.*

MB: In decorating an apartment I like to think about the way you walk in and how one color works with another.

BLDD: *With limited funds, and an unwillingness to live in a bare environment, where do you begin? A few good pieces of furniture, a rug, something to hang on the wall?*

MB: I think you start with the background. I think the architecture is very important: getting the doors in the right place, adding or subtracting any moldings, changing the entrance to a room, perhaps heightening the door or widening it, or adding bookcases, making all the structural changes, then doing the painting of the room, which should certainly be the best paint job you can afford.

BLDD: *Would you do the best paint job before you even bought that one good chair?*

MB: Only because I think if you do a really fine paint job—for example, let's say you spend a great deal of time in preparing the walls, canvasing and perhaps glazing them—it is only going to get better as it gets older. It's not going to have to be redone in five years or so.

BLDD: *Let's get back to our budget friends for a moment. They don't even know if they're going to be in that apartment in five years, and they'd rather invest the money in their possessions than improving their landlord's property. With what should they start?*

MB: If there's a change to make architecturally, then it's a nice thing to do. None of us wants to spend a great deal of money and then leave the results behind for the landlord. If in fact you can't make architectural changes or don't want to, then you work with what you have. In one of these modern buildings, paint everything—the ceiling and walls and woodwork—the same color, either a light or a dark color. Then buy the best possible upholstered pieces you can afford at the time, because your upholstery becomes the bones of the room. These are the things that you're going to have for a long time, to work around. After that you add your tables and lamps and chairs. When you think about decorating on a budget, no one really expects to finish a house in a set period of time, except people who are not really sure about who they are and what they're all about.

BLDD: *When you are working on a job, where do you prefer to work? For example, do libraries do it for you, or bedrooms, or dining rooms?*

MB: It's the bedroom that I like the best. I like pretty bedrooms. I think bedrooms are terribly important. It's a place where most people spend more time than they really think about, or imagine they do. If you're city people, you come home from a tough day at the office. And if it's a very gray city, you want to come home to a very cheerful kind of an apartment.

BLDD: *What's the ideal bedroom for you?*

MB: I think it must have a large comfortable bed, preferably a

canopy bed. I personally feel there's nothing nicer than a canopy bed. It's just a nice way to wake up in the morning, and fall asleep at night. There's something about waking up in a big king-size bed in the middle of a room that makes you feel as though you're in the middle of nowhere. And there's something about waking up inside of a canopy bed that makes you feel . . . not back to the womb, but back to a cozy, defined space.

BLDD: *Are you of the unmade bed—I mean, in the sense of non-bedspread—school?*

MB: Exactly. I think it's wonderful to have all the accoutrements, the bedspread and all the various nice things if you've got someone to undo them for you every day. If you have to do it yourself, I think it's not terribly pleasing. I hate coming home very tired in the evening and then having to undo the bed and find a place to put all the pillows and the bedspread. It's much easier just to hop in.

BLDD: *Are there desks or dining areas in your bedrooms?*

MB: There haven't been any dining areas to date. But there usually is a sofa in the corner, or in a bay window—where one could have breakfast and perhaps entertain. The idea of eating and sleeping in the bedroom is one I don't find terribly attractive myself. But a lot of people eat in bed watching television if they're alone. I don't think I'd like to entertain in my bedroom, and then have to use that room as a sleeping room.

BLDD: *Have you given up on dining rooms? Do you think they're no longer as relevant as they once were?*

MB: No, I think if you've got the space, they're wonderful. It's a great luxury in New York today to have a dining room. A lot of people are taking their dining rooms and turning them into dining room-libraries or sitting rooms. I think that's a very good idea. In a New York apartment where you're limited to maybe three or four rooms, a dining room is a waste of space, unless you entertain a great deal.

BLDD: *Lots of decorators have given up on curtains. They think of them as something of another period, because of the*

Mario Buatta's living room
Collection of boxes

difficulties of maintenance and the grime of city life. Are you one of those?

MB: No. I think curtains are very important. I think they become an architectural element of the room. For example, if a room doesn't have moldings, if it's totally devoid of anything, a pure, square box, curtains help soften that space, and they can help soften the lines of a room. I hate to tell you this, but a lot of people who haven't been using curtains are finding out a lot about drafts and cold. So with the energy shortage, curtains will be coming back. In the same way, color has suddenly come back. A lot of interiors are being done with pastel furnishings. The white and black and white and gray room is becoming a thing of the past, and color is suddenly coming in. All of this is terribly important. A lot of architects and designers and decorators never sway; they have a point of view that becomes very inflexible. And they don't realize that you can't be a star today and say, "Well, this is the way it's going to be." People won't take that. People want to be treated as though you're working for them and you're doing what they want and what's going to make them happy.

BLDD: *If one of the purposes of the designer is to help people, how do you keep from intimidating them with all that good taste? The professional decorator is considered a repository of good taste, whatever that means. What does that expression mean to you—what is good taste?*

MB: Good taste is a very loosely used expression; I think that what is good taste for you is not necessarily good taste for me. If you feel that you look great in a blue room, or a gray room, and that it's right for you, then it is. Who am I to say that it isn't right?

BLDD: *But isn't that part of your professional role, to make a judgment and to give advice?*

MB: I can give advice, but if people don't take it, there's nothing I can do about it.

BLDD: *We know that there are regional differences in taste, but are there regional differences in good taste? For example,*

54

Mario Buatta
Canopy bed
1975

you've done jobs in Ohio, in Michigan, and so on. Do you find varying interpretations of good taste?

MB: I think the magazines have done a great deal to influence people in the way they want to live, or the way they think they want to live and it has nothing to do with the "real" them. I think good design is more important than good taste. It's easier to put your finger on what is good design than on what is good taste.

BLDD: *What is good design?*

MB: Something that's pleasing to the eye. Something that functions well.

BLDD: *You are a very cheerful fellow, and your clients like that. They feel comfortable in your presence: obviously that is part of your whole technique and style.*

MB: It's the actor in me.

BLDD: *I assume, too, that there have been areas of disagreement and compromise. Has anything ever occurred that would cause you to leave a job or have you ever been "excused" from a job?*

MB: Yellow butterflies and blue and white paper all over a room!... That was one of the things that did it. If you come to a point with a client where you realize that you're just not going to see eye to eye, if they don't understand what you're doing or what you're trying to do and you don't understand what they're thinking, then there's no point in going on. It's like a marriage that doesn't work. And in decorating, this rapport between a client and a decorator is terribly important. Most of my clients go back seventeen years, to when I first started. I'm still working for these people.

BLDD: *A good part of your work, then, is not only taking on clients, but redoing the work of ongoing clients.*

MB: Exactly. I'm still adding to those jobs, bettering them, changing them.

BLDD: *You emphasize beautiful patterns, chintz, floral designs, classical furniture. And, in spite of the fact that we are in this so-called post-modernist era, you must seem, to* some critics at least, somewhat old-fashioned. Are you ever called that? And if you are, how do you react?

MB: I've been called a lot of things, but never old-fashioned. I've always stuck to my own point of view. I first studied architecture at Cooper Union. But I decided I hated math and I hated the whole idea of building. I remember looking at some of my old high school textbooks a few months ago and I used to draw pictures. I guess I used to be a daydreamer: I'd draw pictures of houses I'd seen and I'd change the windows. I was always fascinated by architecture. But I really didn't like what it was all about, the essence of putting it all together.

BLDD: *Have you ever collaborated with an architect on an assignment? How does that work out, and who has the final say?*

MB: It depends. If I call an architect in to work with me, he knows that I want it to be the way I want it to be. So he'll help and try to carry out my thoughts. When you're working with an architect and a client, and you're called in after the architect has designed the house, it can be a disaster, because you're stepping on his toes. I remember a client came to me and showed me the plans of her house. It looked like something out of Disneyland. I've never seen so many arches. I finally ended up calling it "The House of Falling Arches." There were six arches! And the proportions were wrong. So the architect became terribly offended. I decided not to work with the client, because I thought he would be impossible. The client has had several decorators in, and she's called me back since. She said, "I'd love to have you take a look." And there's just no point, because I don't feel that I could help her. She really knows what she wants in that house. And she's going to make a mess out of it. And she's going to do a good job of it.

BLDD: *We've said a few words about what a Mario Buatta interior is known for. Perhaps you could tell us what you think the hallmarks, or the identifying aspects, of a Mario Buatta job are?*

MB: Usually mass confusion. It takes me a long time to get

started. You try to get inside the mind of your client. When I was younger and had a great deal more time, I used to spend a weekend at a client's house. I'd learn to live the way they lived. I'd learn what their movements were—if they were out playing tennis on Saturday morning, if they would have an early breakfast, and whether they liked breakfast in the breakfast room or if they preferred to use the dining room, or the kitchen, or whatever. All of these things became terribly important—their sleeping habits and so on. I don't have the time to do that any longer.

BLDD: *So now you tell them when to play tennis . . .*

MB: I don't mean that I'm a dictator. But you get to know they way the family lives, and how they use the house. One of the most important things, I feel, whether you're buying or building a house or an apartment, is to live in it for a while and get the feeling of what you like—whether the sun comes in this window at that part of the day and you migrate to that room or another room, or whatever. And to learn to feel it. There's no point in buying a house, decorating it, and moving in the next day. You may hate it.

BLDD: *Why don't you tell us four or five things that we would recognize as the hallmarks of your sensibility if we walked into a Mario Buatta room?*

MB: I would like to think that it didn't look as though I did it. I'd like to think that it looked as though the people had some help but they—rather than one person—really did it.

BLDD: *There are some recurring themes . . .*

MB: I would say color is one. I like to use lots of colors that are pleasing to the eye. I like them to kind of blend, so that the effect becomes something like looking into a garden and seeing that though lots of things are happening at one time, there are no discordant notes. Although those happen from time to time, too! Comfort, I would say is another. I'm a great advocate of very comfortable rooms—rooms that look as though you want to sit down the minute you walk in. Certainly, it's important for the personality of a client to come

forth for a room to look like the person who lives there even though you may not agree with what he or she has. I guess I would say the two main themes are comfort and color.

BLDD: *And collections?*

MB: Well, not really, because everybody doesn't collect, and collections are not a part of every room. It's nice to have a client who has a collection and has a point of view in that respect. But then again, it can also be very difficult, because collectors are very difficult people. They like having their things exhibited in a certain way. It's either an intellectual collection, or they're collecting for the sake of investment.

BLDD: *Do you find more of that happening?*

MB: Collecting? Yes. Very much so.

BLDD: *Is that in furniture, or works of art?*

MB: Both works of art and furniture. But it can be detrimental to a room. You find that a client has suddenly brought in an antique shop, and you don't know what to do with all the pieces. He has pieces from all different periods, or seventeen chairs that don't fit into the room. And you wonder what you're going to do with them all. It's not an easy job being a decorator.

BLDD: *There must be some jobs that you've done that especially please you. Which ones would you most want to be known for?*

MB: I love my own apartment, and I like the job I'm working on at present.

BLDD: *Is that your Detroit job for Henry Ford? Can you tell us a little bit about it?*

MB: They live in England part of the year, so they like the feeling of the English country houses—lots of color, fresh flowers, warmth, a roaring fire, and all that sort of thing that makes a house work so well.

BLDD: *How involved are those clients in the design and decoration of their house, and how flexible?*

MB: They are very involved and very opinionated, but very flexible. You have to be flexible, you have to be willing to hear someone else's point of view. This is what I meant about a decorator needing a decorator. I'm involved in so many things and I see so many fabrics, so many colors, so many pieces of furniture. There are so many things that I come across every day, things that might become a part of my life, be in my apartment. So it's nice to have someone come along and say, "I think it's great, but I think maybe you ought to do X, Y, Z," or whatever. You may not take their advice, but it's nice to know that somebody else sees it a different way.

BLDD: *In another room in your home-office, you have done what a decorator should do for a client. You have samples of every imaginable textile or fabric or rug that reflects your taste. Why don't you describe what that room is like, and why you've set about to make this little inventory of fabrics and textiles and rugs and wall surfaces.*

MB: First, let me say that I have a small staff, not only because I like to do things myself, but I think that when people hire you they like you to do it yourself. They don't want someone from your staff. My personal feeling is I can only wear one suit a day, eat one meal at a time, drive one car, live in one house. I don't really want to knock the world down. I think there's plenty out there for everybody. And I want to be happy in what I'm doing. And there's no point in trying to do too much, and not doing it well. Because I think everything needs time, and I need time. My work is my life. I work seven days a week, and I don't think of it as work. Let's get back to my nerve center: it's a little thing that I learned years ago, because I've always worked out of a closet. All these years that I've been in the business I've had tiny closet areas to work out of. This is my first chance to really have an office, and to spread everything out. Over the years, everything just had to be terribly organized—plastic boxes for everything you could think of. Each of the plastic boxes holds every kind of material that we use, whether it's samples of wood, glass, fabric, window shades, window blinds, or paint. And all of these things need to be in one place where you can find them. In

that particular room, all the things are organized by color. All the paints are grouped by color, all the fabrics are together by color. And all those various sorts of pillows and objects that I might need to finish a room would be there—to sort of help things move along swiftly. But it has to be organized. Organization is very important. But the biggest problem in our business today, of course, is the trades. There aren't the people to execute the work today. But there are a lot of young people today doing things with their hands, and I think that what's happened lately has been remarkable.

BLDD: *One of the things that struck me about your workshop is that it appears to have evolved over a long period of time. This implies that decoration is not fashion, that colors do not change, that there is no great shift in emphasis. Is that the way you feel?*

MB: Yes. I've never changed. I've had the same chintz in my sitting room, with the dogs, since 1962. I've moved four times, and each time I moved I just added onto the curtains—either this way or that way. They're like old friends.

BLDD: *Are you that enterprising with your clients' curtains, as well?*

MB: Oh yes, absolutely.

BLDD: *So many people revive periods. The '50s and '60s seem next. Where will you be then?*

MB: Right here in the '80s.

BLDD: *What's the longest assignment you've ever had?*

MB: Seventeen years—there are houses I'm still working on; people change things, add to them, acquire country houses. As to how long it takes to complete a job, down to the last detail, I don't think that is ever possible.

Mario Buatta
Living room
1971

Mario Buatta
Living room
1978

Mario Buatta
Bedroom
1980

Mario Buatta
Bedroom
1975

Mario Buatta's living room
two views
1978

BLDD: *Angelo Donghia, one of the best known contemporary designers, is a custom designer for the elite; he is also a designer of furniture, sheets, wallpaper, and glassware for the mass market. He is a unique combination that encompasses most everything—from wall coverings to celebrity interiors. What was it that attracted you initially to the world of design?*

AD: Probably the most important draw on me was to live more attractively, to make the world a better place to live in, and to know that when people feel more attractive, they just feel better.

BLDD: *In a sense, you are, like some of the best-known fashion designers, a household word. You design custom-made objects and at the same time make commercial products to be sold to a very wide audience. Thinking of that, and looking at the way you are put together, did you ever consider going into fashion design?*

AD: My father was a tailor, and I grew up with him wishing that I would follow in his footsteps. Oddly enough, I have nothing to do with fashion. Last year I was asked to do a collection of women's blouses, and I said no. I have no desire to do that, and I don't think I ever will.

BLDD: *Without extending the meaning, or placing too much emphasis on one phrase, you've just said that you have nothing to do with fashion. Isn't there an aspect of fashion in interior design?*

AD: That's incorrect usage on my part, saying, "I have nothing to do with fashion." Of course, most everything has to do with fashion. When I used the term "fashion," I meant "clothing."

BLDD: *You were an apprentice to your father for some time. Did that have any influence on your choice of career? How was your early interest in decoration nurtured?*

AD: I think just by looking. I can answer your question directly: Kaufman's Department Store was located in Pittsburgh, the closest place to the town where I was born that had anything of the nature of a city. Kaufman's did beautiful windows and beautiful room settings. I was attracted by that, and for some reason, I wanted to do it. That was probably when I was about eight years old, and it's never changed. I met the president of Kaufman's once, and I said, "You know, I always wanted to do your windows when I was growing up." He said, "Well, any time you're in Pittsburgh, please stop up." But I haven't yet.

BLDD: *What made you decide to, and when did you, leave that small Pennsylvania town in which you grew up?*

AD: I left in 1953, when I was eighteen. And I never went back, except to visit relatives, of course.

BLDD: *You left to come to school, and soon after school, you started your interior design career. That's more than twenty years ago. You first worked as one of Yale Burge's assistants. How did you get that job and what did you do there?*

AD: After I left the Parsons School of Design where I was trained, I decided I wanted more degree credits. At that time Parsons had no affiliations as it does today, so I went to New York University. On New Year's Day, I decided that I would like to start working. I had been going to school for some time and wanted to get a good start in life. I still had one course to complete, an elective called "Real Estate." But I didn't go back. I made three phone calls—to Yale Burge, Billy Baldwin and Michael Greer, in that order. First I called Yale and he wasn't in, but his assistant was, and I was interviewed. I was dressed up in a Brooks Brothers suit, and I had my button down shirt on, and a tie, and I looked very appropriate, but somewhat more like a banker than a college student. I walked in and they said, "Terrific. You'll come back and see Mr. Burge in about a month. He's in Mexico." So I came back exactly when they said to, and Mr. Burge said, "How do you do, young man? What would you like to do?" And I said, "I would love to work." He said, "How much do you want to make?" I said, "Well, I'd like $100 a week." He said, "You'll take seventy-five." I said, "I sure will!"

Angelo Donghia

BLDD: *How important is formal training to the career of an interior designer? Can you learn to be one—since, in a sense, it is not a science, but an art?*

AD: That is a very difficult question to answer. It is not a science, yet it has rules. We're speaking of a very sensitive subject—creativity. I feel many people are capable of doing what I do. You are capable of doing what I do. Some of us are born with a lot of fences. Sometimes a school helps break down those fences. I interview many people, and I now have over seventy-five people working for me. They come to me with their portfolios and tell me where they've been trained. I barely read the resumé. I'm not interested. Most important to me is, what do they love? I want to know what they like, not what the school has taught them to like. I want to know just how they feel about things. So I'll say, "What have you seen recently that interested you in a magazine or in some theatrical production?"

BLDD: *What kind of answer are you looking for—what kind of reply would engage you?*

AD: There has to be some alignment with my point of view. I don't speak to them dictatorially and say they must do it only my way, but I do give a certain direction, so that there is an ease in working together.

BLDD: *There must have been a great "ease" in working with Yale Burge. After three years at that first job, you were named a vice president, and, by your sixth year, you became a partner and the firm was renamed Burge/Donghia. What influence did working at Burge have on your own style and the way your career has evolved?*

AD: Yale Burge was a very good friend of mine; he had a great effect on me. He was like a second father. He was a great businessman; my father was a great businessman. Burge had incredible integrity, and was very kind to people. He was very kind to me. And I learned a lot from him. I didn't necessarily align my point of view with his. We were kind of separate, although, while we worked together, I tried to include his point of view within mine. As we grew further apart, as he stepped away from the direction of the company and I took over, I began to blossom and formulate the approach which most people know me for today. As a matter of fact, it is the approach I started with at Parsons and it's what I picked up again after my separation from Burge, though I didn't really separate from him, he just did other things.

BLDD: *One of the things that you're best known for is what makes your practice different from that of so many other interior designers—the large scale of the business and the expansion of your own design work. When and how did that begin to happen? What was the first of your ventures?*

AD: Yale had a number of other interests; he had a reproduction French furniture business, and an antiques business, as well as the interior design business. I was a partner only in the interior design business. That's what I meant when I said that he separated and went on to other things. But he was a very fair person. He wasn't out to get everything he could get from me. What he wanted was for me to direct the company and make a profit and to do it with the quality and integrity that he insisted on. When I did that, I was certainly satisfied that he had his company, but I too began to feel restless, because I like to do many things. I can't do one thing; I like to wear many hats. For example, I met a young man—his name was Seymour Avigdor—who designs fabrics. He had presented them to Mrs. Parish at Parish/Hadley and she loved them. Then he presented them to other designers, and they loved them, too. He told me, "I'd love to get them printed, but no one will print them." And I said, "Look, Seymour, I'll start a company, and I'll print them for you." So we developed a company called Vice Versa. This company is know today as Donghia Textiles, with Vice Versa remaining a division. We not only carry those original designs, but others as well. That was my first project. I asked Yale to be involved in that business, but he said, "Look, do it yourself. It's yours, and now we'll be balanced. I'll have my things, you'll have your thing, and we'll

65

have our one thing together."

BLDD: *Other than the fact that your friend came up with a good idea, what did you find lacking in existing fabrics or furniture that made you want to strike out on your own?*

AD: I'm a gambler, I have a very free spirit and I believe in trying anything. I have a great belief in my ability, a great belief in myself, and I always think of something. My attorney always asks me, "What is the worst thing that could happen? What is the worst thing that could happen if we got involved in 'X' project?" And I always think of that. The worst that could happen would be that I'd fall on my tail, and I'd get up again. I strongly believe in taking chances and risks in life—in every way, and in every direction. Woody Allen says that in order to succeed you must have the willingness to fail—that's a very strong statement.

BLDD: *You are such a disciplined person, in your work and in your private life—in everything you do. It all seems so ordered. So it is something of a surprise to hear you talk of risk-taking. I suspect, however, that the margin of chance is very minimal, by the time you execute your ideas. It is apparent in your office and in your work that it's all very carefully thought through. You said earlier, in fact—in contrast to the comments of most of the other designers with whom I have spoken—that there were "rules" to interior design. There must be rules, by the way you play the game. What are some of them?*

AD: The three rules that I have, with respect to the profession, are: keep your agreements with your customers; keep your ethics; let people have what they have coming. A lot of people get into our business just to receive, but it's very important to give, also. There are a lot of nonprofessionals in the interior design business; there are a lot of people out there selling merchandise, or getting something for someone, wholesale. But I'm speaking of the interior design business as a profession and as a respected one, where a designer can really give his customer what he or she is paying for. That's the first

rule. The other rules have to do with the process of decoration itself and there are many of them.

BLDD: *You're contrasting the amateur with the professional interior designer. How do you differentiate between decorator, space planner and designer—how do you define what it is that you do?*

AD: I am a decorator and I am a designer. Sometimes I decorate and sometimes I design. A lot of designers today want to be called interior designers only. I find it is very bad for our profession that they do that, because I feel, "What's the difference?" In designing, one really takes care of the whole matter, the spaces, the conceptualizing. In decorating you may do any degree of surface decoration, playing with skins. That's how I would use the word "decoration"; it is still a design process.

BLDD: *Do you find that some of the people in your profession are defensive about the term "decorator" these days?*

AD: Yes, And it creates bad public relations for our profession.

BLDD: *Why are they so defensive about the use of the word "decorator"?*

AD: Have you ever heard a mother say, "My son, the decorator"? I doubt it. I am constantly out on the road talking to various professional organizations and schools, trying to get my message across. It is my attempt at upgrading the professionalism in our business. One way is to handle ourselves as professionals, and not as business people. There is a difference. I'm not saying that one can't be the other, but one has to be a professional first—to be regarded as a professional—and then a businessman.

BLDD: *You are one of the people who has managed to be both a designer-decorator and a businessman. In fact, I think you were the very first interior designer to put your name on a mass-produced line. Wasn't it sheets? How did that come about?*

AD: A friend of mine at Bloomingdale's said, "You should be designing sheets." I said, "How do you do that? I'm an interior designer and I'm a decorator." He said, "I would like to speak to somebody. I'll call you." In about two days, I had a call from J. P. Stevens. That was ten years ago. I created my first collection then, and my first sheet design was called "Good Morning, Glory."

BLDD: *Flowers?*

AD: Yes. And then there was one called "Rainbow." Then I did my most famous sheet, which was called "Windowpane." We revived it again, this year. Big companies like J. P. Stevens, or any large manufacturing company, always look at yesterday's statistics to see how they can make more money. Looking back on "Windowpane," they discovered we sold $8 million, at cost, in one year, of one colorway.

BLDD: *What did you learn from the J. P. Stevens operation that you apply to your own design business?*

AD: I learned that you need organization at all times in order to get your product out, and that you must have a perfect management setup in order to produce properly and fulfill your commitments.

BLDD: *You have designed a great number of things, including sheets, towels, tablecloths, bath rugs, wallpaper, and, of course, beautiful furniture, glassware, and china. Which do you consider your most important product?*

AD: Furniture is my first love. And I'll tell you the probable reason for that: it might be that little hidden command, way in the background, to be a tailor. Furniture is the closest thing in the interior design business to tailoring. A chair has certain features like tailoring; in a sense, it has seaming.

BLDD: *Obviously, your success cannot be described simply, and obviously, too, it is incremental. But I wonder if you could point to one or two things that you would describe as the "key" to the whole thing. Was there a critical period for you when it all came together?*

AD: I think the turning point in my whole career was when I was asked to do the Metropolitan Opera Club. It was about 1966, when Harrison & Abramowitz designed the Metropolitan

Opera House at Lincoln Center. Billy Baldwin called me and said, "Would you be interested in doing that room?" Of course, Billy has always been my great idol; I have always looked up to him. For him to recognize me at that stage of my life was very important to me. Billy said, "I'll have the committee contact you." About two days later, fifteen limousines rolled up in front of my office. Out came all these very fancy benefactors of the opera. I was very impressed with myself, I have to tell you. I saw them all come in and realized they wanted Angelo Donghia. And I couldn't believe it. I had only been decorating for seven years. Burge himself was extremely impressed. I learned something important from him that day. I went in and said, "Yale, look—we're going to be able to do the Opera Club. Aren't you excited? What a prestigious job!" And he said, "Yes, it's wonderful." He was very supportive, but immediately realized how much it was going to cost him. He said, "How are you working this?" And I said, "Well, we'll give them everything at cost; we'll provide all the drawings, we'll supervise the installation, and we'll do a normal decorating job." He said, "That's fine. Angelo, I'm not going to tell you how to do it; you have a very good business mind of your own. But I'm going to make a suggestion. I think you should charge them."

BLDD: *Did you?*

AD: I said, "But, Yale . . ." And he said, "Uh-huh. They will think more of you if you do charge them." So, I went into that meeting, and felt, "Oh my god, how can I do that? How can I charge these people?" And when I finally got the job, I was still thinking, "What does he mean; how can I charge these people?" But I would have charged anyone else. I was so impressed with getting the job that I was forgetting why I was doing it and why I was in this business. So I said, "You will have to pay the fee." And they said, "Fine."

BLDD: *Has there been room for public service in your life since then?*

AD: Yes, of course there has been. But the Opera Club was a

lesson. I still did it for almost nothing. But I can say that there was greater respect for having charged them. It was a lesson that I never forgot.

BLDD: *How does that lesson affect your career? How do you apply that to your private clients, for example?*

AD: I do nothing for nothing. One of the diseases of our profession is that there is a tendency to become very social with clients. You're doing their bathrooms and their bedrooms; nothing is more personal. I feel that I must keep away from *any* socializing with *any* clients. I make it my practice not to have dinner with them and not to have lunch with them. I could count on two hands the number of times I've had lunch or dinner with clients in the last twenty years. I have decided that the best policy is to keep everything on a business level.

BLDD: *When I asked you earlier what your most important product was, I thought you might reply, "service." How do you establish that special rapport, and how do you keep clients feeling that they are getting enough attention, particularly when their friends have just come from a cocktail party with, or are having as next weekend's houseguest, the person who is doing* their *interior design?*

AD: I just deliver. I give them what they've come for. I'm not interested in becoming their friend. I have nothing against them—there are a lot of people I have worked with whom I would like to have as friends. And after their jobs are finished, we have become friends. But I'm speaking of the period during the process of decorating. It's very important to keep at arm's length, so their respect is on a business and professional level. You would not go out and have cocktails with your doctor. It's very important that clients take what I'm saying as a business arrangement, and not a friendly conversation. But I deliver what they've come for. I have satisfied many people. And I call them every day. One thing I always do in my business, and train the people who work with me always to do, is answer the client's calls. They are never to

leave a phone call unanswered at the end of the day, even if it's midnight. And they are to call all their clients once a day, in order to let them know they are being handled properly. The trouble starts when a client feels he's not being handled properly and is not getting his money's worth.

BLDD: *This regime sounds rigorous, but it must work, because in talking with the people who work with you, I discover that many have been with you for the almost twenty years that you have been in business. You must be doing something right.*

AD: I've always been disciplined. It's easy for me to be on time and it's easy for me to do the various things that I commit myself to. If I decide not to eat a lot, I don't. I have a very easy time keeping agreements with myself, and it has always been that way. It hasn't been learned.

BLDD: *Is there* anything *that's tough for you?*

AD: Sometimes concentrating for long periods is tough for me. I have a hard time sitting still. My mind operates so quickly—it moves faster than my body, you see. My body is here and I'm up there. I could do twenty things at once if I had more bodies.

BLDD: *You manage to do many things now, including your custom design, mass-marketed objects, and furniture. There are a number of things—certainly some of the furnishings—that you have designed on a custom-made level that are also mass-market wares. Do your clients ever object to the commercial availability of certain Donghia designs?*

AD: I have that fear. A lot of people who advise me have had that fear. They've thought that if you start getting in the mass market, people with a lot of money who want prestigious goods are not going to come to you. But the opposite has happened. My business has tripled because of it. It's true that some clients might not come to me, but all those who wouldn't have heard of me otherwise will come.

BLDD: *Do any of them feel that the mass marketing reduces the value of their custom-made furniture?*

68

AD: I don't think so. People know that there is the Rolls Royce and there is the Jaguar, that they are two different things.

BLDD: *How do you assure clients that what is in their custom-made interior is not going to appear in furniture showrooms and department stores throughout the country at a fraction of the cost?*

AD: It might appear. But you can't think of it that way. If you think of that you're going to box yourself in. You have to allow yourself to believe that there are more people than the people in this room; there are more people than the people in this city. And there are more people than the people in this state. I have traveled around this country many, many, many times. I have done seventeen cities at one time. I have done thirty cities at one time. This country is very large. We in New York think that the country stops here; there's a glass wall on the Hudson River, and no one else exists out there. But there are a lot of things happening beyond New York.

BLDD: *With all that traveling about, you must have some ideas about transportation. Have you ever designed the interior of an airplane or an airport?*

AD: I have not designed anything for TWA, but I have certainly done Lear jets. A lot of my clients who are major corporate executives have Lear jets, sometimes several.

BLDD: *Do you design the interiors of private planes in living-room fashion? What do they look like?*

AD: You can buy a jet that's decorated by Lear, or they will find someone for you, or you can have your own advisor come in. A lot of architects do that for Lear or other companies. It's a fascinating thing, because it's like designing a yacht, or anything at sea. Space is at a premium and textiles must be inflammable so you have a lot of restrictions. The challenge is very great.

BLDD: *One of your most ambitious and unusual projects to date has been the total redesign of a very grand luxury liner, the S.S.Norway, formerly the S.S.France, a Caribbean cruise ship. You were responsible not only for each stateroom, but both dining rooms, the disco, the cabaret, every table, every table lamp, napkin and glassware. How did you become interested in this particular project—is the sea of great concern to you?*

AD: If you think astrologically, I am a Pisces; I always think of that. I had never done a ship. And, as I said earlier, those fences that limit our abilities have to be removed. One of the fences that had to be removed, in this case, was the fence that said, "You cannot do ships." I removed that fence and I did one.

BLDD: *How large is that ship?*

AD: It's three football fields long, almost nine hundred feet. It has 1,000 staterooms, twenty-six public rooms, three swimming pools, a gymnasium, a theater and endless miles of corridors.

BLDD: *Had you ever been on a cruise before you took on this assignment?*

AD: Never. But I had been on the *Liberté*. I went with the Parsons School of Design in 1957, on the then traditional trip, with my professor Stanley Barrows, who was responsible for a lot of the ability that I gained. I saw Stanley the other night and I said, "Stanley, how nice it was to do that ship—because I remember my first trip on the *Liberté* in 1957." I was in a room with five others, in third class. And he was in first class. We used to sneak up at night and have a lot of fun, and get free beer.

BLDD: *Was there an organizing theme, color, or principle that you used? When a ship is named the* Norway, *it's difficult to picture something that looks like Brazil.*

AD: With all due respect to Norway, it's a lovely country but it does not exude style. You wouldn't think of it as a place to be inspired by. It was difficult. But I had to remember that the ship would be in the Caribbean. It was going to be filled with people in bathing suits and shorts and white clothes and perhaps evening clothes. So it was designed as a background for

69

that activity, against the color backdrop of the Caribbean—the blue of the water and the sky, the green of the trees, the white of the clouds.

BLDD: *What colors did you use?*

AD: Very soft, dusty pastels; salmons and turquoise were the base. These were colors that seemed appropriate for the background. Fabrics were especially constructed for the ship. Most contract fabrics and public chair fabrics are done in wool, but I couldn't imagine a woman in a thin dress or a man in shorts sitting on woolen fabrics. So we developed a special cotton chenille weave that was appropriate, and fit all standards. It was really quite an exciting thing to do.

BLDD: *You* can *imagine people sitting on wool, or at least surrounded by it, in many of your other interiors. One of your trademarks is the men's suiting fabric, the gray flannel that covers walls in many of your interiors. In fact, it lines your own office. Does your use of that fabric relate to your tailoring background?*

AD: I never thought of it that way, but it could. Gray flannel has always been one of my favorite suitings; I wear it a lot. About ten years ago, I was in a gray flannel suit when we were redoing the offices, and I said, "Golly, I just can't think of what to do with these walls. I don't want them white; I don't want them beige; I don't want to cover them in sailcloth." And I looked at my suit, and thought, "Well, gray flannel: what could be more neutral than silver gray?"

BLDD: *Are there any other personal trademarks that we should know about?*

AD: Fat furniture. People always call me "the maker of fat furniture." Someone from the *New York Times* who was once interviewing me asked, "Why do you do fat furniture?" And I couldn't think of anything to say, so I said, "Well, it makes fat persons look skinny. If you sit in a fat chair, you look thinner than if you sit in a skinny chair."

BLDD: *What are the most dramatic changes in design that you've observed in the past twenty years?*

AD: People are beginning to relax about decoration and be more honest.

BLDD: *How does that manifest itself?*

AD: People feel that they don't have to have what other people tell them to have. They are beginning to believe in themselves a little more. It comes with all this "me generation" and with really trying to find themselves.

BLDD: *Does that mean that they need the services of a professional designer more, or less?*

AD: Less, I think. But we can't just say "people," we must qualify this. There are those who will always need interior designers. The size of the projects they undertake could never be handled by anybody but a designer. Then you speak of the mass market. The introduction of mass-market or designer-designed products helps make it an option for people to choose what's right for themselves. I always say to people, "Nobody knows better than the client what he would like."

BLDD: *What about the amount of furniture that people use? It seems to me that some of the "clutter" of the '60s became sparser in the '70s, and the next period may be a happy balance between the two. But it seems that with more and more interest in furniture, there is less furniture being used.*

AD: I think that is true. The big theory that has always been my credo is, "Less is more." I didn't invent that; it came out of the Bauhaus. But I believe in it. People are beginning to see, because of the cost of everything, that they had better start thinking about how much they really need. It is nice to be able to stop when you're halfway finished, because that's when you really are finished.

BLDD: *I've been thinking about what you said about fat furniture, and I think your furniture has a certain voluptuous quality to it. It's soft and warm, and I think it has a kind of billowy modernism, without any of the hard edges. Is that a fair way to describe it?*

AD: I think it's sexy, if I may.

BLDD: *Is that your intent?*

AD: It's what comes out; it's what I do. It's my Italian part.

BLDD: *What are the most neglected parts of the decorating process?*

AD: Ceilings. Did you ever walk into a public room, or into anybody's house, and look at the ceiling? Most designers think that nobody ever looks up, and therefore put everything that they don't know what to do with on the ceiling.

BLDD: *What do you do about ceilings?*

AD: I consider ceilings the biggest lesson I learned while at Parsons. When you study traditional design and architecture of past periods, you sense that the ceiling has been given the same amount of consideration as the walls and the floor. I always think of a room as a six-sided box. If not all surfaces are given the same amount of attention, you have a problem. That box must have your full attention on all surfaces before it's a complete design. If that rule is adhered to, the furnishings within it are only incidental.

BLDD: *Thank you for that rule; I'm now encouraged to ask you to share some other of your design secrets. For example, how do you make a ceiling look higher; how do you brighten a dark room; or how do you make a boring box—the sort of thing that so many of us are surrounded by at work or at home—into an interesting space?*

AD: Ceilings should always be higher. And in order to have ceilings look higher, it is always best to have the ceiling the same color as the wall. The deeper the contrast between the two, the more the eye will define the height of the room. So, in order to keep your attention away from a low ceiling, you diminish the demarcation between ceiling and wall. Then it will appear higher.

BLDD: *Do you do the same thing with the woodwork?*

AD: That's correct. Also, create as many vertical lines as you can; that is an old design rule which goes back to the Egyptians.

BLDD: *You employ that rule with doors—I've rarely seen you do a room in which the door is not the full height of the room.*

AD: Full-height doors and apertures are a popular method of architects today. I believe in full-height doors. It adds to the quality of a room. For a few dollars more, you can have a very custom look by doing that.

BLDD: *You talk about that few dollars more, but not everyone is a corporate executive, or a Barbara Walters, a Ralph Lauren, a Diana Ross, or a Halston—some of your clients. Do you still have the time to deal with a client on a small budget?*

AD: No. It sounds as if I don't want to do it. I would like to help everyone. But I have a lot of people working for me, I have my own survival, and the survival of all the people who work for me, to think about. It is not good business for a company that is set up to do large jobs to do small jobs. It takes more time to do the small jobs than it does to do the big ones. And, with the kind of time that you'd have to put into handling people who would like to have your services, there would be no profit and, eventually, no business.

BLDD: *Let's say someone comes to you who is a close friend, or a niece or nephew, the kind of client to whom you can't say no. They have more taste than funds, and they want to bring the Donghia style into that little room on which they have little money to spend. What would you tell them to do? Should they begin with furniture or rugs or paint or art?*

AD: You have no idea how many people ask me what they should do. I'm always grateful when they don't.

BLDD: *But when they do, what do you tell them?*

AD: I try to be kind. I'm not about to dismiss people because they've asked me a question. I give them as logical an answer as possible. Most people think you do that and you have solved their problems. I usually turn it around and say, "What do *you* think you should have?" And they say, "Well, I like . . ." Then they should have that. Because that's true, you see. Everyone really knows. If you would ask me that question, you would know the answer for yourself. You know what you want. People are very strange. They want your advice, but they want you to tell them what they're thinking they want.

71

AD: Clients are looking for agreement all the time. The more you agree, the more you've got them eating out of your hand.

BLDD: *You offer people financial arrangements different from most decorators, particularly on the scale and budget that you deal with. Can you explain that to us?*

AD: I'm of the feeling that one shouldn't corner anyone. I don't like to be cornered. I feel more comfortable when I'm given options and therefore I feel that giving options to others works out very well. I don't say, "This is how I work. I don't do it any other way, and this is my fee." I've developed three different methods. One, by making purchases and collecting the difference between wholesale and retail. Two, by charging flat, fixed fees. Or, a combination of the two. And, finally, an hourly charge, starting with perhaps a couple of hundred dollars an hour for my services.

BLDD: *Are these arrangements worked out in advance?*

AD: Yes. They're all contractual payments. Businessmen prefer that. Businessmen whom I work with say, "I don't believe that you're really giving me the opportunity! Now I can ..." One of the greatest problems of the interior design business is that people always feel something's going on that's hidden.

BLDD: Is *there often something going on that's hidden?*

AD: Did you ever see decorators in a showroom, saying, "Is it the list or the net?" They create all these secrets. You're probably wondering, what are those decorators doing? Are they making money on the side; are they making a deal; could I get it cheaper somewhere else? Are they trying to sell me a whole bundle of goods just to make a profit? That fear has riddled our business. We should be up front as designers, and we should say to the customer, "I would like a $100,000 fee to do your house." Because in a lot of cases, that's what it comes out to on a sale-of-merchandise basis. If that is the case, I feel the designer would be saying to the client, "I'm worth $100,000." I am. Clients would have more respect for us, the mystery would disappear, and our professional status in the community would be better.

Angelo Donghia
"Windowpane" bed linen
1974

Angelo Donghia
Living room with "Fat" furniture
1976

Angelo Donghia
Living room with custom
furniture
1975

Angelo Donghia
"Madison" arm and side chairs
1972

Angelo Donghia
Renderings for S.S. Norway
completed 1980

78

Angelo Donghia
Staircase
1975

Angelo Donghia
Living room
1975

BLDD: *Joseph Paul D'Urso is widely known as a master of minimalist design. Clients know what they won't get when they seek his help. Joe, perhaps you can tell us what it is they will get. What are the hallmarks of your design and for what is your work best known?*

JPD: First of all, I would like to think that my clients will get a lot of my attention. My interest in working with interiors, especially with residential projects, is to try to establish an ongoing relationship with the client. A design has to evolve; it's not the sort of thing that you can resolve completely on paper. I think the relationships I have with my clients are probably what I enjoy most about my work.

BLDD: *You don't just leave it as "less is more"; there's always a deeper philosophy to what you do. Your designs offer a background for living, a nearly but not totally neutral background that permits the personalities of your clients to come through. Minimalism, you say, doesn't reduce individuality, but enhances it. Is that accurate?*

JPD: I don't know that a neutral background is really an accurate description. I prefer to use the term "architectural." When my clients come to me, they have recognized that their space has to be transformed. It may be an interesting space, but it doesn't work for what they need. It may be a space that has exciting elements about it, but was designed for the family or social structure of the '20s or '30s. Or more often, it's a space that is problematic or anonymous. Life and excitement have to be breathed into it. Certainly one wants a space to be exciting, dynamic and provocative. But at the same time, it is a design, not a painting. You're not completing the picture; the client has to add that which really brings it to life. It's not unlike a stage set, I think, where the action of the play really makes the set important—it makes it make sense. Unless you see it in use, the design is incomplete.

BLDD: *What do you do when a client has a great number, or even a few, beloved antiques or paintings—objects that one doesn't generally associate with your approach to design? Are you willing to work around existing objects and furniture?*

JPD: Usually people come with a real need for a professional service. I don't think people need to fix on any one or two or three things. Very often, this kind of fixation is an indication that they are frightened of the process they have decided to undertake. It's a human thing to hold on to something familiar until you have something new to grasp onto. Often people cling to things until, after the space is realized, they no longer need them. They eliminate many of the things they thought they needed on their own. But I love to have clients who are obsessed with particular things—as well as those who are obsessed with having very little.

BLDD: *Is it a strong point of view that interests you?*

JPD: It's the fact that they really know about and care about their things; they mean something. They're not just sentimental objects that get in the way. I question people: I say, "Do you really want that, do you really need it, do you understand that perhaps it is not a good example of what it is?" People often think they have a real Tiffany lamp when it's only a poor reproduction. I think if you can expose people to the real thing, they're likely to make a different judgment.

BLDD: *Is it ever difficult to convince clients to simplify not only their living spaces, but their possessions and presumably, as a result of that, their lives?*

JPD: I think this is what we all want; it is why people consult a professional designer. They're coming for the discipline that's involved and to try to establish priorities and to organize elements that may have become disorganized at various points. They're really trying to key their lifestyle into a space that perhaps was not designed to be lived in that way, but has advantages they want and need.

BLDD: *What's the process like? How do you urge, or perhaps even insist, that they edit their possessions?*

JPD: I don't insist. Usually they come to me with that already done; they've gone through a very thoughtful process. I don't think I'm the kind of designer that someone just picks out of

Joseph Paul D'Urso

the phone book and rings up without any idea of what their involvement will be, or what my services will involve.

BLDD: *How do you get your clients?*

JPD: The best clients come having seen or spent time in a space that I've worked on. Often, they're friends of clients and have been able to see the whole process, the before and after.

BLDD: *Twice you have referred to yourself as a designer. Many of your colleagues identify themselves in different ways: while some call themselves designers, others describe themselves as decorators or space planners. Where would you place yourself on that spectrum? Is there any real difference in those words, or is it just a question of semantics?*

JPD: It's a question of semantics. It's always a question of semantics with a word or label, but it's the quality and the result that really matter. I can think of a lot of people who called themselves decorators in the past who did much better work than ninety-nine percent of the people who call themselves designers today. So it's irrelevant as far as I'm concerned.

BLDD: *How do you identify yourself?*

JPD: For a lack of a better term, I think "designer" is perfectly valid. It suggests a certain openness to the total environment—to dealing with all aspects of it, technical, visual and functional.

BLDD: *Obviously, some sort of collaboration must take place between the designer and the client. What commitment do you expect from the client in this process?*

JPD: It's definitely a collaboration. I think the collaboration can go as far as the client is willing to go. Obviously, different projects require different kinds of collaborations, depending on the scale and length of the project, for instance, or whether you're living in the same city. I like to keep the whole thing rather loose. I get definite ideas quite quickly about a project, and I often present my solution to a problem shortly after I get the project. But I always like to keep it loose; I like the client to be comfortable with that approach.

BLDD: *They've obviously come to you as the professional because early on you do make that judgment or decision. So on the one hand, they want your help, and on the other, they want to be part of the process. How does that all coalesce?*

JPD: Ideally there's an element of trust, and then the role of the designer is very clear—you are providing clients with a service. You listen to them, and you fulfill their needs in a much more interesting way than they ever thought of. The more clients see of what the problem is and how it can be solved, the more they understand about the whole process of making design decisions.

BLDD: *One of the ways you've solved problems is to reduce the complications. How does the almost clutter-free environment that you create measure up to the disorder of contemporary life? Is it possible or even desirable for most people to live as cleanly as a D'Urso design would have them do?*

JPD: It's interesting you should use the word clean, because I had an experience with a friend recently who, for various reasons had to move back into a much smaller apartment. For years she had sublet the apartment and was now really unhappy with the space and the way it was furnished. One evening, just spontaneously, we decided to tackle it and see what we could do. I started pushing things around. I pulled everything away from the walls; there was quite a bit of furniture. As we pulled the furniture back, things started to fall away—pictures that were stashed there, boxes and so on. We were able to eliminate a lot of things that she didn't even realize she had. After working for a couple of hours she said "You know I can see now that this is not only a more logical, but also a cleaner way of living. It's because you can actually *see* everything." I think there's something to be said for that. If one isn't careful, one ends up living in a storeroom, because there are so many things that we're all intrigued and fascinated by, things that we find ourselves owning, or suddenly being responsible for. And if you have a limited amount of space, as most of us do, you really have to discipline yourself.

81

BLDD: *How do you help discipline the client now that the collecting urge, be the objects precious or sentimental, seems to be more widespread than ever?*

JPD: It's a matter of making a choice. If you want to hang something on a wall, then you no longer have a blank wall. If that blank wall provided a certain calm or serenity for you, and you decide to put something on it, the effect of that object should be equal to, if not more than, what was there before. You have to constantly be in touch with your environment and constantly question yourself: why am I putting this here; why is that right for me? By doing that, I think you make decisions that are right for you. It's carelessness and lack of involvement that leads to clutter and bad design. It's not a question of there being many or few things in a space, it's where they are and how they relate to one another. You can go into someone's environment and it can be almost empty with a couple of flowers, and that can be very exciting. Someone else's space, filled with books and objects, whatever, can also be very exciting. Because the environment is felt, it's real—it's not that one is cluttered and the other is minimal.

BLDD: *I guess most of us are so caught up with the business of living that we don't stand back and look at the way we live. Then suddenly we see that it has evolved.*

JPD: Yes, I think we fall into traps. You go to a museum and you see an exhibition that excites you so you buy the poster and put it on your wall, maybe because you think the wall needs something, but more likely because there is nowhere else to put it. Or you have a corner that's empty, so you go out and buy a plant because you saw in a magazine that a corner of an apartment should have a plant. We're under pressure all the time to conform, to fill space and to justify things in material ways, rather than appreciating pure space or silent moments in space, or being content with the memory of having seen that exhibition.

BLDD: *Not all of us are quite so disciplined. But, assuming you're not opposed to the purchase of that poster, is there* room *for it in a D'Urso design? How can the design evolve and grow?*

JPD: I would like to think that my clients will be sensitive to the fact that a wall is of a certain proportion and is filling a certain function within the whole. Putting the poster on the wall changes that. Is the change for the better—is it something that you really care about? It's not *what* the change is, but whether one cares about it enough.

BLDD: *Is your style especially suited to any particular style of living, a particular age or economic group, or kind of situation? Can anyone live in a D'Urso interior?*

JPD: I don't think I have a particular style. My range of clients has been very wide, both families and single people. I really think I have succeeded in solving individual design problems as they come along. My decisions are not arbitrary. They're not preconceived according to a style. I don't start out by saying, "You have to have this and that to create my certain style."

BLDD: *But certain things are considered the hallmarks of your design: a kind of spareness, the use of industrial materials, glossy white walls and dark gray interiors—wouldn't you characterize these as typical of your work?*

JPD: Yes, I suppose so, but only if you look at it that way. I think that you have to analyze each project separately. I do this with each of my clients. They want to know if ideas are going to work. Often, you make similar decisions that make sense. And then you go on to other decisions. I have done many apartments in New York in a certain budget category—budget is a very important aspect of what goes into making a design—so you will of course find similarities. But there are as many dissimilarities—the really important things that make a space unique, and particular to a client's needs. Yes, there's gray carpet here and there, but I think that's almost a nondecision: it allows you to go on to something else more interesting.

BLDD: *These backgrounds of yours have sometimes been*

described as "neutral." What does neutral mean?

JPD: Neutral is an easy word that is too often used. Neutral suggests "bland"; it suggests a lack of commitment, I don't want to think that my spaces are neutral in that sense. They are meant to be inspiring and should generate some kind of communication with their occupants.

BLDD: *Does this clutter-free environment that so appeals to you resemble in any way the kind of environment in which you were raised, or any environment to which you responded at an earlier time in your own life?*

JPD: I don't think so. Traveling has been incredibly important to me—seeing and being exposed to other ways of doing things. In this country, more than anywhere else, perhaps because we are so physically isolated from other cultures, we tend to do things a certain way. When we eat, we eat at a table, and it's thirty inches high, and we have a dish and a knife and a fork and so forth. I was able to experience many other ways of doing such things. These experiences have been my sources of inspiration.

BLDD: *How do you eat, if not at a table with a knife and fork?*

JPD: I usually eat on the floor. Or I eat out in a restaurant or at a friend's house. Those are basically my ways of eating.

BLDD: *You have recently designed a number of pieces of furniture. No producer of furniture has longer been identified with good design than Knoll—the folks who manufactured the Mies chairs and the Saarinen chairs. You have helped to re-form and recharge their identity in their new Venturi and Rauch designed showroom, with some of your designs. In fact, you are the first young designer they comissioned to do new furniture. Can you tell us something about what you have created for them?*

JPD: I believe their intention was to widen their market in the residential area, and I was fortunate enough to be one of the people involved at the beginning. The products that I've designed for them were aimed in that direction, although, as with anything else, there are no labels on them that say you shouldn't use them in an office or any other particular space.

BLDD: *Can you describe for us the square tables and sofas that you designed for them?*

JPD: The products are categorized in three different ways. We have what we call low tables and high tables, which really mean lounge-height tables or dining/work tables, and lounge seating. I'd consider all of them to be systems based on the function that each is filling. The lounge seating can be obtained in several different configurations. It is a very relaxed, informal approach to a sofa; the depth and the pillow arrangement is casual and more physical, I think, than many other sofas on the market.

BLDD: *Can that sofa also be a bed?*

JPD: Yes, it can be. The seat width is thirty-nine inches, the width of a single bed. You're meant to relax. I think that any-one who's not willing to relax would have a hard time on my sofa. I've noticed people in the showroom sitting on it too cau-tiously; if you are self-conscious or a little bit awkward, you might have a problem with it. The idea is to sort of attack it—I think that's good. I think it will function best in a situation where the person has gotten accustomed to it and is really using it. The high tables, again, are a system, but there is a very wide range of shapes. We have many round tables, but we also have a square table, and a rectangle with rounded ends, which we call a "racetrack." It's an attempt to analyze the problem of a table, and to offer as many choices, within a carefully controlled vocabulary, as possible. We have mate-rials ranging from plastic laminate to wood to marble and stone. So you're really able to choose what you think is appro-priate for your particular space. We've sold a lot of high tables. What's interesting to me is that even though we have other materials, so many models have been ordered in black.

BLDD: *How do you explain that?*

JPD: I think that people are responding to the understated purity of the shape, the detailing and the proportions. They don't want something that's easy and tricky and jazzy.

BLDD: *That's your first experience, as far as I know, with any kind of large-scale manufacturing. What's it like for someone as disciplined and philosophical and as precise as you are to work with a commercial manufacturer—to try to combine the practical with the esthetic?*

JPD: My big experiences in that regard were with Calvin Klein. The Calvin Klein menswear showroom was particularly interesting. Because it was a company in formation, I was involved in a good deal of the planning. This was interesting because I think that the space they chose, and its design, really did influence and change the way the business was organized. It was a very unusual situation for everything to be happening at once. We were all able to sit down and decide how best to express in physical form the needs of showroom space, office space, and public relations space.

BLDD: *Did you have a similar experience with Knoll?*

JPD: I just designed the furniture, not the showroom. The introduction of the furniture was an opportunity to place the furniture in that space. That was perhaps more interesting to me and much more rewarding even than designing the furniture, because the way furniture is used is what interests me.

BLDD: *You're particularly fond of industrial objects and a kind of industrial esthetic. How did you first become interested in the use of such materials?*

JPD: It was really the inability to find enough from the normal sources. Design is not a vending machine where you push a high-tech button, a post-modern one, or whatever. When I first started working on my own, we had catalogues from all the different furniture firms and hardware companies and so on, and in them were very few products that I felt were worth using. So I started looking elsewhere. The design market has been very badly influenced by consumerism and has gotten off the track. It happened a long time ago, and I think it got to the point where something else had to happen. That point, for me, was simply saying that there are other sources for a fau-

cet, or a chair, or a light fixture. And often, these sources were really much more on target, because they were not trying to make one feel cozy, or warm, or any such thing. They were made to work, so they were good design.

BLDD: *What is most important to you then? Is it function, is it comfort, is it esthetics—or perhaps all of them?*

JPD: The decision-making process is such a mystery; you never really know why you want to use something or own something. I'm speaking of myself as an individual now, not as a designer. You have different things for different reasons, and you're willing to put up with different things for different reasons. As a designer, obviously I'm very interested in comfort, I'm very interested in function. But again, comfort is very subjective. It's what is appropriate for that particular situation. A chair might be comfortable for a particular task, but might not be comfortable for me to live with, because it's not the way I live.

BLDD: *How do you live? What kind of D'Urso design have you created for yourself?*

JPD: I think the most important thing is to find beautiful spaces. I have found beautiful spaces. In New York, I have a list of requirements for my ideal space: high ceilings, a fireplace, sunlight, are all very important to me. I enjoy these things. Other than that, I haven't really been able to shape the environment in quite the way that I would if I were in a different economic situation. But I have a very beautiful space, architecturally.

BLDD: *I guess it's spatial complexity that most interests you in your assignments. Let's talk for a moment about a specific design: for an apartment in an older building on West Sixty-seventh Street in Manhattan. Were you tempted to strip the old detail? Did you perceive this job as one of cleaning up or space manipulation?*

JPD: That project was exciting because it was a powerful space to begin with. Again, it was really the budget that determined the way we approached the design. It was a very limited budget on which we had to do a lot. Even if I had wanted to rip out all the moldings and expose the more basic structure of the space and deal with that, it would have been out of budget range. To me it is so important to understand the appropriateness of every aspect of the project, to understand the client's financial commitment to the project. It's very important to get that clear at the beginning, so that you get things built, so you don't design things that are just fantasies and then suddenly get the construction bids and find that they're three or four times what they were supposed to be.

BLDD: *What does a D'Urso job cost today? Does minimalism cost less, or does the term "minimal" apply only to the eye—and not to the pocketbook?*

JPD: Again, I think it depends. I've done whole apartments for a relatively small amount of money. Sometimes I tell younger people forty or fifty thousand dollars for an apartment and they say "My god, it's such a lot of money!" But it depends. It's all relative.

BLDD: *That is a lot of money.*

JPD: It sounds like a lot until you start itemizing things and you see where it goes.

BLDD: *Because of your architectural training, you're also involved in a lot of lighting and heating and air conditioning, and things of that sort.*

JPD: I can be, but I don't have to be. You can light an apartment with one light, or you can just have candlelight. It doesn't have to be elaborate to be beautiful. What's important is understanding what you have to work with at the beginning, and then carving it up in a way that you feel will make it work.

BLDD: *Let's come back to some of those industrial objects that you've used for more than a decade. Do they have the same meaning for you now that they had when you started to use them?*

JPD: I'm trying to think of how many industrial objects I've used. I can't think of that many; perhaps certain drawer units or certain light fixtures.

BLDD: *Table bases, containers, light fixtures . . .*

JPD: But again, they're not industrial so much as they're simply designed without arbitrary decoration. They're not trying to be styled elements—they're just basic straightforward designs. There's nothing new about much of that.

BLDD: *We talked about how special the space was in that West Sixty-seventh Street apartment. Do you prefer that kind of space, or the modern high-rise apartment where the space is more neutral and you might have a greater opportunity to create the kind of design that would represent your intentions?*

JPD: The nice thing about being busy, about having ten projects, is that they're very different, so you can have everything. You're working on a big apartment with low ceilings; you're working in an old building; you're working in a brand new one; you're working on one that's not even built yet. Personally, I usually relate more to older buildings, because they have character, and a certain quality of construction, and you have a structure that you can knock around without the thing falling down on you. On the other hand, I think what's exciting about living in New York is to have a great view—if you can find it. There aren't many old buildings that have that. There are some, perhaps, along the park, but I'm talking about forty stories up in the air, the kind of thing that you find in Chicago.

BLDD: *You work alone now, but you have worked with Ward Bennett, and I know he was a great influence on your career. Can you say a word or two about that, and about his significance in American design today?*

JPD: I think Ward embodies the concept of total designer—someone who is interested in every aspect of the design process. I've always thought that was something to aspire to. I've known Ward for a long time now; a lot of the exposure that I've had, in traveling particularly, was largely due to my working with him and being a friend of his. I hope it shows very positively in my work today.

BLDD: *How did you come to know him originally?*
JPD: I went to see about working for him after I graduated from Pratt. I remember he said to me, "Why don't we try this for a month or so and see how it works." It worked out fine.
BLDD: *How long did you work for him?*
JPD: I don't really remember. It was strange, because it didn't seem like a job. Ward doesn't work that way, ever. And I don't remember that I worked that way. I got involved immediately in several interesting projects, new houses. Then I went to England for a couple of years and continued to work on some of his projects. It was very loose, and it just sort of evolved.
BLDD: *Do you work that loosely now?*
JPD: Yes, I think I do. I have an office where there's someone answering the phone and making sure that my clients know I'm still around. But I like to just walk out the door and wander off.
BLDD: *Have you ever worked in partnership with another person, and would you like to?*
JPD: I share an office with Bob Bray and Mike Schaible; doing our office was a collaborative effort that worked very well. We had a good time doing it.
BLDD: *Why don't you describe the turn-of-the-century Beaux-Arts building that you work in. What has it been like to share space with Bob Bray and Mike Schaible for more than a decade? Their work is in the same spirit, one might say, as yours, but do you work on jobs collectively? How does the situation work?*
JPD: I think it's a very healthy situation. I like activity, and I don't see myself in a big office or even a small office, working alone. I often do much of my design work either at home or traveling. I don't really need that much quiet; at least I don't think so. Maybe I do and don't realize it. The office is an exciting environment. The space is very beautiful; we have beautiful light and a beautiful view.
BLDD: *Has working in such close quarters exerted any influence on your work? What have been the rewards of this kind*

86

of intimate working relationship?
JPD: I'm sure we influence each other. It would have to be that way with friends. And we share many of the same sources of inspiration. On a practical level, it makes a tremendous amount of sense to me to share space. I would not be able to afford that space if I didn't share it.
BLDD: *Let's talk about sources of inspiration for a moment. I know that you're heavily influenced by architecture and art. Are there any particular sources that you invoke?*
JPD: I suppose native or indigenous architecture: architecture without architects. I'm talking about a Japanese house or Egyptian architecture of a certain period, or Italian hill town architecture; architecture that has evolved slowly and with a real relationship to the way of living in a certain climate using materials of the area. I think that's been a very strong influence on me. But so have, I suppose, the designers at the turn of the century who were dealing with interior spaces in a very intimate and total way. There are many of them. I'm constantly going back, looking at their work, more than anything as a reassurance that it is possible to do something extraordinary—that you can have something that's an ideal situation and it can get built.
BLDD: *Your recent work has begun to evolve in a way that incorporates more objects—an occasional old piece, for example. Do you feel yourself moving in a particular, or a new, direction?*
JPD: I like to think that each new job is a new direction. How else can one approach it, really? You just don't know what's going to form the program for the next project. The client and the particular job are really what make the project what it is. If there are going to be objects in the space, or if there's going to be art, it's not because of me, it's because of the client. It is my responsibility to deal with these things in a serious and functional way, and to present them in the proper perspective.
BLDD: *What's the best and/or the most satisfying job you've ever done?*

JPD: The one that comes to mind is the Calvin Klein menswear showroom. That was truly exciting. I really lived and breathed the project; I was there practically every day for the four or five months it was under construction. And it was a very complicated project for me—up until that point I hadn't done anything nearly as large.

BLDD: *It was quite a departure for Seventh Avenue at that time. What gave Calvin Klein the courage to do it?*

JPD: I don't think he thinks about things in that way. He does whatever he thinks is right and exciting at the moment.

BLDD: *Are there any jobs that you've done that you wish the design books would forget, and that you would like to forget as well?*

JPD: No.

BLDD: *Modernism has now become a classic style. Do you feel that you are designing in a historic period style when you do a modernist interior—almost like a designer who creates an eighteenth-century room?*

JPD: It may be a weakness on my part, but I don't relate to that kind of dialogue. I don't philosophize about what I do; I just make what I think are the appropriate design decisions for the project. I don't think of design as being of a specific period.

BLDD: *It your approach really more spiritual than art historical?*

JPD: Yes, that's my point of view. Other people may be interested in trying to analyze the source for this or for that, but I am not an academic in that sense. Obviously I'm very interested in architecture of the past. There's so little today that's really fantastic. But on a philosophical level I don't think too much about it.

BLDD: *One impact of inflation and spiralling construction costs is that most of us are only going to be able to afford a smaller house or smaller apartment. Over the next twenty years it has been predicted that the way we live will change very radically. How do you think we can scale down, without sacrificing our human space needs and our own individuality?*

JPD: I think that there has to be, and there will be, a challenge to the direction new construction is going in today. I focus immediately on the concept of the window, and what windows have degenerated into in most speculative buildings. I think we're almost at the point where people will not tolerate this direction any more.

BLDD: *What recourse do we have?*

JPD: The recourse will have to be a reconsideration of the whole—the economic choices that are made, what money is spent on. Look at the new buildings being built today and the amount of money that's spent on lobby spaces and facades and imported travertine exteriors. I would simplify on superficial levels like that.

BLDD: *Then what, by contrast, are the fundamental concerns when the environment becomes pared down? What do we need?*

JPD: I think we need beautiful windows. I really do . . .

87

Joseph Paul D'Urso
Calvin Klein showroom
1979

Joseph Paul D'Urso
Knoll International
D'Urso Collection
1980

Joseph Paul D'Urso
Living room
1979

Joseph Paul D'Urso
Living room, two views
1980

Joseph Paul D'Urso
Bedroom
1981

Joseph Paul D'Urso
Bathroom
1981

Following page:
Joseph Paul D'Urso
Dining room
1980

BLDD: *Mark Hampton has had a most unusual preparation for his career. He studied history, economics, and law until he changed direction and became an interior designer. Mark, how important was that early training to the work that you're doing now?*

MH: I think it was probably not that important.

BLDD: *Then why did you do it?*

MH: It seemed too unconventional to become an interior decorator. There was no place in Indiana to train for it, no place to work doing it, and until I actually got a job, it seemed an ephemeral kind of career to strike out on.

BLDD: *Here you were living in Plainfield, Indiana, with a population of 3,000 at that time, reading* House and Home *magazine. How did you ever manage to get a copy?*

MH: A wonderful elderly couple built a very modern house in Plainfield in 1950, when I was ten years old. I hung around the building site all the time watching their house go up. It was the only modern house in town. They turned out to be great lovers of Frank Lloyd Wright and Mies Van der Rohe. When Mies' Farnsworth House came out in *House and Home* in 1951, they gave me a subscription to the magazine. Those magazines were my great treasure. I kept them all. I've now cut them up. It was very difficult to vandalize them, but I now have them all filed in boxes according to country.

BLDD: *Were Frank Lloyd Wright and Mies the models who interested you?*

MH: I always liked lots of different things. Even now I like all different styles. I loved Frank Lloyd Wright, but then I loved old houses, as well. I had an art teacher in the fourth grade who taught me the difference between Victorian and Georgian houses, and between Georgian houses and Greek Revival houses. I thought that was wonderful, and I loved drawing all kinds of houses. I never really settled into liking one particular style.

BLDD: *Does that attitude continue to inform your work now, or do you have a particular signature?*

MH: I would hope it characterizes my work. It's almost impossible not to fall into some kind of pattern because people come to you having seen something you've already done, and frequently they say that they like the previous room, and want it turned into a room for them.

BLDD: *It must be flattering that clients come to you because they've seen your last job—but it must be discouraging, too, if you want to go on to your next one.*

MH: I think the thing that's discouraging is to work with a personality who has no confidence, no personal point of view, and, as it turns out, no real taste. There are people who will look at a picture and want that picture. But they have no real sense of their own taste.

BLDD: *What* is *good taste?*

MH: Good taste, I think, is certainly not definable in short sentences. You've got to look back at what periods of taste have survived. I suppose that's why I'm very timid about making predictions about present taste. We can look back at the great modern designs of the '20s and '30s and see what still looks great and what doesn't. You have to trust yourself. I don't think that you can be a decorator if you don't have some awful vanity about your own taste. That's strengthened by people's opinions of you, by your success. It's simply too late to say the Louis XVI chair is bad taste, or the Queen Anne chair is bad taste, or the Barcelona chair is bad taste. We know they have passed all possible tests.

BLDD: *You've had three excellent finishing schools in addition to your own training. I'm referring to the work that you've done with David Hicks, McMillen and Sister Parish. How did you land your first job with David Hicks? That was quite a coup for a first job.*

MH: It was marvelous. He wasn't famous in the United States at all in 1961, when I went to work for him. I was an undergraduate at the London School of Economics. In my spring term, I had very few courses; only one tutorial. I drew all the time, as I do now. So I took a portfolio of drawings along to

Mark Hampton

interview for a job. He was losing his assistant in a month, and asked me to come back, which I did. I worked there for almost three months, mostly doing drawings. Later on, here in the United States, I represented him for almost three years. I was still at the London School of Economics when I began thinking I wanted to go into decorating, and my parents thought it was a terrible idea. So I went back, finished my undergraduate work, did a year of law school, and then went into art history—it seemed a kind of compromise, and sounded more serious to my parents then decorating.

BLDD: *How did you get to interior design from art history?*

MH: I always did interior design in the summers. I always had some sort of decorating job.

BLDD: *One of the places at which you worked was McMillen. One very often hears a reference to the "McMillen canons of good taste." What are they, and are they different from other people's notions of good taste?*

MH: I don't think they're any different; they're much more strict than the canons we now have. The relationship between taste and fashion has intensified in the last ten or fifteen years. I've been in New York for eighteen years. I've seen decorators like Mrs. Henry Parish and McMillen, Incorporated go from very conservative, beautiful, valuable-looking rooms to rooms that are much more strongly stated. In some instances you could even say overstated. I think that I overstate things sometimes, too. Taste is much more adventuresome now. The McMillen canons of taste were, and are—since they still do some rooms like that—very strict. I read a very appropriate line by Nancy Lancaster in a recent magazine, saying that you don't want to do everything up and get it finished down to the last detail. Something has to be left undone. Those McMillen rooms of the '30s and '40s had a wonderful coolness to them. They weren't completely fringed up, or gilded, and the moldings weren't excessive. Right now a lot of decorating is excessive—it's overstatement.

BLDD: *You've said that you, too, sometimes overstate. Why, since you know better, do you do that?*

MH: I'm not saying that overstatement is necessarily bad. It's just chic-er, bolder.

BLDD: *There wasn't always such a thing as interior design. There aren't many great grandmothers around who had interior designers or interior decorators. How old is the profession?*

MH: It began, I think, in the eighteenth century. Then it sort of disappeared; it became the work of upholstery companies. Eighteenth-century French and English rooms were certainly decorated—by cabinetmakers or by architects. You have that incredible phenomenon in England of Robert Adam designing furniture and Thomas Chippendale making it. Or Thomas Chippendale's firm making the furniture that he designed. These men designed curtains, moldings, ceilings, carpets, chairs. In the Croome Court tapestry room at the Metropolitan Museum, everything is designed by Robert Adam, including the fireplace. That is certainly interior decoration closely linked to architecture. Like a lot of things that have to do with taste, it had to do with the expanding economy, the rising middle classes, the *parvenu.* The new rich have had a huge impact on taste. That is where a lot of the overstatement of our time comes in. It's lust for opulence. In the nineteenth century, the huge houses that were built all over England were furnished by the big upholstery companies in London. Even Malmaison was decorated by Percier and Fontaine. Rooms were ordered by the builders of the houses. They would order a finished room, and then see drawings of it.

BLDD: *Design then was only for the privileged, until we come to the twentieth century, and what you refer to as the rise of the middle classes—with a more widespread affluence, mobility and education. What happened from about the turn of the century through the 1930s?*

MH: I think from the turn of the century to the '30s interior decorating was still just for the very rich—the people who hired Elsie de Wolfe and Syrie Maugham, and Frances Elkins

out in California, doing those huge houses for her brother, the architect David Adler. Decorating really started to become an enormous business after the Second World War, with people like William Pahlmann at Bonwit Teller and all the magazines, and the promotion.

BLDD: *What about just before that? What about Elsie de Wolfe? Was her influence widespread? How do you think she influenced the rules of decorating and taste? Would you date the early emerging popularity of design in this country to her influence?*

MH: Yes, but I think even more important was the start of the decorating magazines. Condé Nast started publishing *House and Garden* magazine in this country during the '30s. In those days nobody said, "I don't want to have my house published." If you look at those old magazines, the richest, chic-est people would allow themselves to be photographed in their rooms. It's funny that the people were very innocent about publicity. It wasn't the vulgarity for a lot of people that it is today. Those magazines are what really marketed the idea of having a decorator.

BLDD: *In the 1950s and 1960s that seemed to change too, from interior decorating to interior design.*

MH: Yes, that's a great question, the interior decoration, interior design polemic.

BLDD: *What is the difference?*

MH: For a lot of people, "design" is a real euphemism, I think. They don't like the word "decorator."

BLDD: *Does it have an amateur connotation?*

MH: I think it does. It sounds flouncy, superficial—you know, new lampshades and new curtains and all those things. The point of calling it interior design, I suppose, is that now decorators do what architects and cabinetmakers used to do back in the eighteenth century. The interior decorator now quite regularly rips everything out and puts it back a different way.

BLDD: *How do you define what it is that you do?*

MH: It's very flexible. If somebody comes to me with a big project, and wants to add a wing or tear down a room and make it bigger, I can do that, then decorate the new area and work with the landscape architect on the outside. I love doing that. Conversely, if someone comes to me with a room filled with beautiful furniture and some good paintings, and wants just a good paint job and some new upholstery, I'll do that, too. What I do varies radically from one client to the next. I love going in and just redecorating the room, not redesigning it, especially if someone has marvelous possessions.

BLDD: *I think that there must be a particular kind of client that you would find ideal, since you are so interested in art and antiques. What kind of client do you prefer? Is it the collector that you're most interested in working with, in contrast to other designers, who might prefer that clients rid themselves of many of their possessions?*

MH: Yes, I think I prefer the collector. I sense a great deal of snobbery mixed in with that thought, personal snobbery. I like people who have taste that I find wonderful. That is a form of snobbery isn't it?

BLDD: *Wouldn't you like to help shape and form someone's taste?*

MH: Oh, I certainly do like shaping and forming. But I don't want a parrot for a client. I don't like a client who just says yes, and doesn't know the difference between a good idea and a bad idea. I like clients who have beautiful possessions, want to get more, and who rely on me to improve the looks of their houses. But I like a certain intelligence.

BLDD: *Do you get a lot of good ideas from your clients?*

MH: I get loads of good ideas from some of them and, of course, I get no ideas at all from some, good or bad. That's very difficult. Those clients usually don't last. It's stupid to waste their time. And that does happen in this business. You can work for a certain amount of time and then realize that you can't finish.

BLDD: *Is a job ever finished? Even the ones that you intend to finish?*

98

*Mark Hampton
Entrance hall
1974*

*Mark Hampton
Bedroom
1974*

*Mark Hampton
Rendering for Boucher room
The Frick Collection
New York, N.Y.
1962*

MH: Good jobs, for people with whom you love working, are never finished. Bad jobs are finished when the last bill is paid.

BLDD: *You created a series of interiors in an apartment on Manhattan's Upper East Side that are very much in the manner of an English country house. Do you think that period particularly lends itself to apartment living?*

MH: It does in New York, because a lot of apartments are built in a sort of neo-Georgian style. That's another example of how fashion starts creeping into the whole concept of decorating. It's something that I find difficult to balance intellectually. You do like to be in style. You do not hire a decorator to be out of style. You do not hire someone who is happily out of style. A lot of these New York Georgian apartments were designed as American Georgian houses. It seems quite clear that the English-looking apartment—and by that I don't mean the converted mill or barn, but the rather grand English country house—has become more fashionable now than it was twenty-five years ago.

BLDD: *Twenty-five years ago the style of the moment was French.*

MH: Yes, or else that very arid sort of George III style: you know, gray walls, gray carpet, Pembroke tables, wing chairs. Williamsburg, in the '50s, had an enormous impact on that sort of "Proper Taste." Remember the paint colors when we were little? Williamsburg blue, Williamsburg green, gold. I used to work with a woman who was on the staff at Williamsburg, and she would call those rooms Williamsburgers. It's a wonderfully obvious name for them: the yellow wing chair, the green woodwork, the green rug, the green curtains, and crewel in the den. At any rate, the apartment you're referring to did not begin like a Williamsburger, because the owners only moved in about seven years ago. They moved from a house full of French furniture into this Georgian apartment. We originally did it in a rather chaste Georgian way: white walls and a lot of chintz, but rather cool.

BLDD: *When the particular room that I'm thinking of was*

finished, the walls were a very white white. It looked like not only a very finished room, but a very splendid one, which would satisfy even the most exacting of tastes. However, in a rather unusual turn of events, you and the client decided to change the color of the room when it was all finished. What prompted that decision?

MH: Actually, it was my clients' idea, not mine, but I thought it was a great one. They had lived with the white walls for two or three years and two things happened. It looked too cool to them, too disciplined. And I find that's a great point in decorating. The longer you live in a room, the more sure you are of the effect the room has on you, to say nothing of the effect you have on the room. How does it wear? Is it wearing well? Frequently, a room that's very strict, when you live in it for a long time, starts loosening up around the edges. That can spoil the atmosphere.

BLDD: *What do you mean when you say "loosening up around the edges"? I thought you liked a lived-in look.*

MH: I love a lived-in look, but some rooms don't lend themselves to lived-in looks. I think that's one reason that the beautiful cool modern design of the Bauhaus cannot appeal to an awful lot of people.

BLDD: *And you have certainly never been very high on high tech . . .*

MH: *Never* high on high tech! I've seen high tech rooms that are wonderful set pieces, but they don't have much latitude, to me at any rate. They can't go very far. You've got to put the paper away; you've got to put your book away; if someone gives you something, you've got to put it away. We've all seen those rooms where there is no place for a Christmas gift. For some people, of course, this is wonderful, because some people don't have very lively attitudes toward the accumulation of things.

BLDD: *Let's come back to that white room, when the client had the idea of changing its color. What did you both do?*

MH: First of all, she painted it pink, because a friend of hers

suggested it. These are the sort of things that happen to decorators—sometimes they have nice, happy, funny endings, and sometimes they're the sorts of things that you grind your teeth over for months and months. She was tired of the white walls and they were looking gray, a little dingy, not fresh—lived in, but not right. So she said, "I'd like rosy, flattering walls." People are always saying they want flattering colors.

BLDD: *What* are *flattering colors?*

MH: What, indeed, are flattering colors? It's like asking your decorator to be a make-up artist. At any rate, her friend said, "Paint it pink." She painted the walls pink—without me. It's a vain thing to say, but it really was terrible. Those pink walls weren't right. But this young woman has wonderful taste. The minute the walls were finished, she knew they were wrong and she called me up and said, "We've got to do something about these pink walls." We glazed them over to make them a very soft, deep red. I happen to love glazed walls. And they wear very well in the dirty New York air. That's how the whole thing evolved. It really was her idea.

BLDD: *Once you had these cherry-reddish walls, how did they work with the rest of the furniture that was already completed?*

MH: They were terrific. The chintz looked beautiful against them.

BLDD: *Did you rearrange anything?*

MH: We actually left the furniture where it was. Then we slip-covered some of the furniture to make it look softer. We just softened the edges of the room all over. I think it was all caused by an emerging love of clutter, the accumulation of living in the apartment. Clutter is sort of a sloppy word; I don't mean to imply sloppy clutter, but a greater profusion of things.

BLDD: *The kind of room that you prefer is filled with comfortable furniture and personal memorabilia. Where do you draw the line between comfort and clutter?*

100 MH: First of all, I hate clutter that doesn't have any reason.

BLDD: *You really want to organize cluttter.*

MH: Yes. People buy shells all the time—we could all own 80,000 shells. So why collect only five of anything that common? I find it very boring and very cheap-looking. However, if you collect wonderful shells that you find on a beach or are given, that's something else. But just collecting junk because you feel that clutter is the look you want is something I dislike. I hate pointless, impersonal clutter.

BLDD: *Everyone can't afford Tiffany's, and everyone can't afford beautiful boxes or wonderful objets d'art, but would still like to collect.*

MH: If you have original taste, or at least nice taste, you can find pretty and personal things that you can afford. And that, of course, is the best kind of collecting. Some people have books which are interesting to look at, and table tops which are interesting—and they don't have to be covered with things—just simple arrangements of pretty memorabilia, pretty objects. It's also a good reason to hire a decorator. If you know that you can't have vermeil boxes made in the reign of Louis XVI, or marvelous English porcelain, or Brancusis, then you've got to find something else to put on your tables. If you don't have confidence about finding things but do have the confidence to edit them once you're shown them, that's a good reason to hire a decorator. Have him help find things you like.

BLDD: *You've said that you believe in the happy amateur. What does that really mean, and do you really believe it?*

MH: I really do believe it! That's the person with great taste who really likes to decorate. People like that usually are rich, because they have to have a pretty expansive attitude about trying things out, whether they're gardening or upholstering or painting, or raising a roof or lowering a window. They sometimes make mistakes. As we all know, everybody sometimes makes mistakes.

BLDD: *But I think we all know, too, people who have more taste than funds, and somehow manage, by their own vision and taste and wit and education, to put together large and small things that define a space and a personality.*

MH: I know dozens of people who fit that description, as you do. The ones who live in New York are luckier, I think, because you can still get things done there. In New York, anybody can find a nice upholsterer, a good painter, or somebody who will finish up a room. But there are towns all over this country where you literally can't get anyone to come in and finish your floors. You can't get someone to come in and paint your walls, unless you accept someone with a bunch of latex paint and a roller and a pan and maybe a drop cloth. That's what makes New York so exciting for people in my trade.

BLDD: *You've worked in lots of other parts of the country— Ohio, Texas, California—how do you manage to deal with craftsmen in these other places, or do you move everything in, sort of a catered affair?*

MH: I love working out of town. You do move a lot in, sure. I hate to sound like a prima donna, but I insist on having the curtains and the furniture made in New York; the carpets, too. That is a big undertaking. I have had to fly painters around, too, as have many other decorators. McMillen used to fly them all over the country. There are some places where there isn't anyone who can do the final fancy surface.

BLDD: *You've only been in business on your own for five years, and you obviously have been very successful. But there is only one Mark Hampton, and there are only twenty-four hours in a day. How many clients can you deal with at one time, let alone clients out of town?*

MH: That *is* a big problem. Out-of-town clients, of course, aren't calling you every day. They're not saying, "Get over here, you've got to see what's just happened," or, "You know, there are two hooks out of the curtains."

BLDD: *Does that really happen?*

MH: Oh, sure it does. Of course.

BLDD: *It sounds as if a good part of your time, in addition to being designer and decorator, is spent as analyst and parent.*

MH: And as a furniture repair service. I sometimes feel as if I'm in the maintenance business. Fixing chairs, fixing lampshades, replacing missing parts. It's endless. But that doesn't go on quite as much with a job that's a thousand miles away.

BLDD: *How do you manage those demands on your time? What if someone calls you from about a hundred miles away, someone who lives someplace in New Jersey?*

MH: Or Southampton. You just have to hot-foot it down there and see what's going on.

BLDD: *Is there nowhere geographically undesirable for you?*

MH: I went to Saudi Arabia twice. I thought that was geographically undesirable.

BLDD: *What prompted you to go there?*

MH: It was a huge complex of buildings, for a remarkable man—a prince who is not a playboy sort of prince, but a serious middle-aged man, deeply involved in politics. He's surrounded by an incredible band of followers, minions, sycophants. The whole thing was just impossible. My wife said, as I was fretting over the second trip, "Is it your desire to be the most famous decorator in Riyadh? If not, why are you doing this?" And of course, it was a very cogent question.

BLDD: *You live with your wife, Duane, and your two daughters in a rambling Park Avenue apartment in Manhattan that I think does reflect your love of space and color. How do you live, and why do you choose to live in this fashion?*

MH: The way we live has evolved slowly over seventeen years. We've been in our current apartment ten years. Before that, we lived in a sort of middling-modern apartment, and before that in a two-room, fifth floor walk-up. That was before we had any kids. The modern apartment was one of those places where you couldn't even leave the newspapers out. But I had just gone into business, and—this sounds very crass, but it is a fact—I wanted it to be a bold statement of my decorating. I was working with David [Hicks], and he wanted it to be a bold statement. So it was a bold statement. It was chic and news, and it got published a lot.

BLDD: *Did it have a very David Hicks look—the carpets, the*

Mark Hampton
Library
1970

chrome?

MH: Oh, very. It was the year the patterned carpets first came out. We got the first bale of carpet hot off the ship.

BLDD: *So in some ways, the residence of a designer is also a showplace.*

MH: It has to be, but it is also a burden. That's the great thing that you have to resolve. Over the last fifteen years, we have, I think, resolved it. Though still, we can never be innocent and unaffected about our decoration. I think about it all the time. But you do have to come to terms with what you can live with and what you can't. You see how you entertain, where you put people for dinner, how many books you accumulate, where you spend time. That's what evolves in any home: the knowledge of what you do, how you live, what you can afford. Then you have to add to that your own evolving taste, and, certainly, the power that fashion exerts on your attitude toward taste.

BLDD: *How has your taste evolved in the place in which you live? You say you started out with a very spare apartment. To what did you then move?*

MH: First of all, I fell out of love with plastic furniture.

BLDD: *As soon as you could afford better?*

MH: No, long before I could afford better. We've got a lot of furniture that's junk. You have to be very careful in the selection of your inexpensive furniture. We don't own great furniture; we don't have anything really good. But we have some pretty furniture.

BLDD: *But you could have anything that you want. Why don't you own something that's really good?*

MH: I couldn't have anything I want. The prices on Fifty-seventh Street are astronomical. I would like a big $50,000 gilt mirror—which used to cost $12,000. I remember when they cost $12,000. I have neither $12,000, nor the $50,000 mirror. But I do have a room for books, and comfortable places to sit, and I can bring things in the house and put them down on something. Birthdays roll around, and I keep the things that

people give me. I find places to put them. I love that.

BLDD: *Are there any elements from the original apartment that you've kept in the current design?*

MH: Sure. I love marble and porphyry objects. They're all still there. The upholstered furniture is all still there. You can change the arm on the chair; you can change the trim on a pillow. We've had half the sofas for fifteen years. They're the same, but they could look very modern or not.

BLDD: *In its current incarnation, the living room of your apartment combines cotton print and English bustleback chairs and a Chinese wedding chest and a Victorian desk. How did you mange to bring such diverse elements together and do it with such success?*

MH: We've had the chest since we got married. It's been our coffee table from our first walk-up on Sixtieth Street. Things do look well together if you select them with some sort of taste; it's difficult to explain way. The old example of the French table with the Picasso on it and the pre-Columbian object—we now all know that those things look good together, but eighty years ago nobody did it. There are daring people who make these great strides and discoveries.

BLDD: *Who makes the great leap forward and thinks of mixing those two periods, or those two colors, or those objects on that table?*

MH: Cecil Beaton was one of the great ones. Years ago, I think in the '40s, he did a famous suite at the Plaza. There was a big Léger painting hung over a big Louis XIV table, and a Louis XV chandelier. All the furniture was sort of burgundy-colored. It was a very snazzy room, and very bold. And much copied, for twenty years. Another innovation was Beistegui, whose house was recently published in a huge article. I've looked at pictures of that house for twenty-five years. He had a very bold way. This relates back to the idea of overstatement. I think sometimes those innovative rooms did overstate.

BLDD: *Maybe what you're really talking about is a bold approach. . .*

Mark Hampton
Living room
1974

MH: That's what shocks the eye, you see. That terrific boldness is what changes other people's way of looking at things.
BLDD: *Isn't it often the use of color and fabric that does that, as well?*
MH: Yes, that juxtaposition will do it. Changing people's color taste is a very big stride.
BLDD: *Are we in a period of eclecticism?*
MH: I think we're in a period of great tolerance—a time for both new, bold ideas, and for harking back to old, bold ideas. The Victorian or Edwardian room that people talk about now is a very bold room. Our living room, with all those roses everywhere, is bold.
BLDD: *It certainly is a departure from much of your work. You used more and more fabric, both on walls and on furniture. Does that indicate a new direction for you?*
MH: No. It was a way of dealing with problems I faced. There are some very prosaic reasons for its design. Our living room has no great pictures in it. I wouldn't dream of putting chintz on walls—although somebody like Cecil Beaton would—and then hanging somebody's Claudes or their Fantin-Latours on them. Or Picassos for that matter. I wouldn't do that. That's where I am rather conservative.
BLDD: *Why wouldn't you do it?*
MH: It would look like too much of an effort—too jazzy, too done up, too knockdown-drag-out. But I do think that rooms of the past—if you look at pictures, say, of Stanford White's studio, with a gilt ballroom chair and a Louis XV chair and a Renaissance chair and a skylight and pieces of sculpture—are wonderful! They were very bold rooms. Look at William Merritt Chase's paintings of interiors, which everybody loves. Then there are the turn-of-the-century painters, the American Impressionists. The rooms they painted were very adventuresome. Also, the Japanese craze at the turn of the century inspired wonderful designs.
BLDD: *Is there anything currently that reflects the same kind of breakthrough in both taste and spirit? Or has it all been done?*
MH: Oh, no. High tech hadn't been done, and high tech did break through. But I think once people got the high tech message, there was no place left to go with it. Too many rooms were sort of dead on arrival. The great Proustian kind of *fin de siècle* room is right now a new thing for a lot of people. It's been done forever, obviously; there have always been people who've loved burgundy velvet and deep fringes and pictures of exotica hanging all over the twelve-foot-high walls. But now it's much more marketed, it's much more known. It's getting down to North Carolina, Grand Rapids, and all those people.
BLDD: *How will they translate that?*
MH: Poorly, I suppose. And cheaply.
BLDD: *Why don't we have any great designers designing mass-produced furniture?*
MH: Perhaps it's too simple an answer, but I think the idea of mass anything is defeating to creativity. It so often spoils it. I don't know whether it's because of people's greed for special things, or their need for special attention. I can't think of anything that is mass produced that can compete with something that isn't. What do you love that's mass produced?
BLDD: *There are a number of functional objects—can openers, water glasses, electrical appliances.*
MH: All that German stuff, all that bronze stuff. But those are accessories, bits and pieces.
BLDD: *There are Mies chairs—they're mass produced.*
MH: I love Mies chairs. Huge, and difficult to sit on for a lot of people, but great looking. I had a Barcelona chair. I adored it. I sold it.
BLDD: *How does the design of your apartment let your family live the way all of you want to? I know that your wife has a lot of background in writing about interior design. Does she help make decisions about your apartment?*
MH: Absolutely. She is constantly being asked, "Do you ever get to do anything; do you ever get to say this or that?" Of course. She has an enormous foot (metaphorically speaking)

103

that gets put down on ideas of mine all the time. I tease her about the book stacks in the bedroom that get dusted like tables. The piles are sort of neat, but they've become permanent. And of course, there's her attitude toward coziness: she likes cozy houses, cozy rooms. She's very comfortable with our apartment now. And she has patiently lived in some very uncozy rooms.

BLDD: *What is your favorite room to design?*

MH: A big drawing room, a big living room.

BLDD: *In what period?*

MH: In a grand house of any period, really. I love getting my hands on a house with wonderful rooms. That's the whole point for me. I'm not crazy for new ideas. I would love to work in a great modern house. I *have* worked in some wonderful modern houses. But I still always love to have another chance to work in a big, beautiful, old room.

BLDD: *What do you do when your client has a collection of paintings and drawings, and lots of objects?*

MH: You simply begin at the beginning. I've worked for some people for years who have gobs of things that Louise Nevelson has made for them, some big Stellas and other huge modern canvases. All their rooms are big, but the rooms have been kept very unfabric-y—no curtains, no patterns, no chintz, no patterned rugs. In a room like that, if you have space and wonderful art, you deal with furniture in soothing masses that are also convenient for sitting. I have a great dread of rooms that are uncomfortable to sit in. It's bogus for people to stand around in rooms that really ought to be sat in. So if a modern collection does exist, you approach it simply from the standpoint of what looks best with modern paintings. If it's little eighteenth-century or nineteenth-century paintings, then you hang them differently, and you use different colors. Some people have old paintings and want modern furniture; some people have modern paintings and want antiques. You're constantly having to try things out. You get better at it the more often you do it.

BLDD: *Have you ever had a failure, a job that you wouldn't want to claim?*

MH: No, though I don't mean to sound self-congratulating. I've had rooms that I had to fix.

BLDD: *What did you fix in a room, when you have had to have a second thought?*

MH: I've had to rip up patterned carpets that had people seeing double and just looked awful. I've had to repaint walls that turned out the wrong color. I've simplified curtains that were too elaborate. These things happen.

BLDD: *How does the client feel about those revisions? Some of them must be very expensive.*

MH: Sometimes it ruins the relationship, and sometimes people say, "Ah, well, it's not your fault. I approved it." That is sort of like being patted on the head, but you are grateful when somebody says that. Frankly, I like working for people who take some responsibility for making the decisions. You don't go to a restaurant and order a meal and say, "I don't like it, take it back." Some people do, I guess, but I don't. You've got to take some responsibility. That trust is the basis of the relationship between the decorator and his client.

BLDD: *Who is the ideal client?*

MH: The ideal has good taste, a compatible personality, a sense of adventure, is rich. A little bit of "Well, let's try it and see how it goes . . ."

BLDD: *You said before that interior designers get better the more often they work, and the more jobs they do. But that need not be the case with furniture. You said once that some furniture was ravaged by time rather than enhanced by it.*

MH: Sure, plastic tables for instance, or those square-looking sofas of the '50s with funny little chrome legs that actually are quite comfortable but look too stiff and strict, so that people don't like sitting on them. I hate that kind of furntiure. It's the same with Danish modern.

BLDD: *Whatever happened to Danish modern?*

MH: I think everybody finally identified it with motel furni-

104

ture and that was the end. I mean: *out*. Also, everybody identified an awful lot of modern furniture of the '50s with offices. Obviously, there are millions of rooms with wonderful strict furniture. But for the most part, people do not like furniture that reminds them of an office. I'm always working for men who want their offices to look like a room at home. That's another whole problem: how to make a man's office cozy.

BLDD: *Why only a man's office, Mark Hampton? What do you consider the most pretentious, or bogus aspects of design? What's the worst mistake that one can make?*

MH: Slavish adherence to what we all call a look, or a statement, I think. We all talk about making a statement. I don't, but I'm constantly hearing about "a statement." "It doesn't make a statement."

BLDD: *What does that mean? Every room makes a statement, positively or negatively.*

MH: I'm talking about degree. The big, loud, noisy, fashion-oriented statement. Does it look like an ad in *Women's Wear*, or an ad in *Architectural Digest?* That, to me, is bogus, and poor. So are rooms that don't look at all personal or comfortable, or inviting. They just don't look as though people with any intelligence could possibly live in them. People who look silly in their clothes and people who look silly in their rooms lack intelligence. They are the kind of people who serve funny food—fad food, fad flowers, fad hair. I could go on and on.

BLDD: *What do you consider to be the best of the American design tradition?*

MH: There's a funny sort of Puritanism about American design, like so many American things—an absence of that European, frightfully rich, upper-class look that is kind of gagging, I think. The most wonderful thing about American art and design is its nice throwaway quality. I hate to see that lost.

BLDD: *You've also talked about that unique American phenomenon—people who are "obsessed with housekeeping." Won't you please expand on what you mean by that phrase, and how it contrasts with what you describe as this throwaway quality?*

MH: It can occur in very simple people; it doesn't have to be a sort of extravagant obsession.

BLDD: *When you say housekeeping, do you mean tidiness and a need for order, or just getting everything matching and lined up?*

MH: I don't mean that at all. I mean that love of cleanliness which really becomes a luxury. In New York, we all know that great cleanliness can become a luxury. It's really nice when the woman or the man who has achieved this doesn't brag about it all the time. I know people who have a wonderful immaculateness, who will describe themselves as though they're quite sloppy, which I think is an amusing kind of self put-down. I know a lot of decorators, and have worked for people who are really unbalanced about cleanliness.

BLDD: *Has it made you more or less organized or tidy?*

MH: Funnily enough, it's made me more organized and more tidy. I do love cleanliness. I think that the longer you live in New York, the more seduced you are by the clean *anything.* If it's clean, you already like it better than something that isn't.

BLDD: *How do you reflect this interest in order and organization and tidiness in a design? I think one of the functions of the professional is helping those who perhaps lack the training, the predisposition, the compulsion for order, or discipline to organize not only an environment but, in a sense, a way of life, by creating a kind of grid for life. Do you see that as part of the function of design and designers?*

MH: Sad sounding, isn't it? Dreary, but it probably is a function of designers. It's the gloomy side of designing for people, the kind of nervous side. I do think that you have to help people to avoid looking arbitrary, trying to look different just for the sake of being different. A love of beauty—beauty one can *live* with—is the driving force behind good decoration.

Mark Hampton
Living room
1976

Mark Hampton
Living room
1972

Mark Hampton
Library
1980

Mark Hampton
Living room
1976

109

110

Mark Hampton
Library
1972

Mark Hampton
Library
1976

BLDD: *Sarah Tomerlin Lee has recently completed her twenty-fifth hotel project, and is now working on the interiors for seven hotels in New York alone. What makes her even more unusual is that while she has long been known as a magazine editor and an advertising executive, it wasn't until ten years ago that she ever designed a public space. Sarah, that is really quite astonishing. What made you decide to take that leap and what gave you the courage to change careers?*

STL: My husband had a fatal automobile accident. At the time, he was under contract to do a hotel in Toronto, then called the Inn on the Park, across from the City Hall. I was his vice president. I was just the vice president to sign checks when he was out of the country, but the hotel people didn't seem to realize that. He had an excellent staff, and we completed the contract. We were also starting the Rye Town Hilton; I did tell the Hilton Corporation of my role, and that I didn't want them to be chivalrous. If they didn't trust me, I would tear up the contract.

BLDD: *What gave them the courage to trust you—as an instant designer?*

STL: I don't know what happens to make people change their minds. At that meeting, they said they were going off to have lunch and would come back and tell me what they had decided. But someone in our group must have spoken with them, because they turned around, took their coats off, and said, "We're going to teach you what we know."

BLDD: *Was it difficult to make the transition?*

STL: I was very nervous on the first job, but I had my husband's wonderful, cooperative staff, so it's not such a miracle.

BLDD: *How does your office function?*

STL: We have four major designers and me. Each one has an expert architectural draftsman. We have a very capable staff so we're not that rushed. We get things done on time, and have time to develop concepts and think in a different way about every project.

BLDD: *Twenty-five hotels sounds like a lot of hotels.*

STL: It's been ten years, and we haven't always done the entire hotel. For instance, with the Helmsley Palace, in New York, we did not do the bedrooms.

BLDD: *Here you are, a genteel girl from Tennessee, who went to Randolph-Macon College in Virginia and majored in Latin and Greek. What in this background prepared you for a career—either in publishing, as editor-in-chief of* House Beautiful, *managing editor of* Harper's Bazaar, *and beauty editor and copy editor of* Vogue, *or in advertising and merchandising, as a vice president of Lord & Taylor, and consultant to both Helena Rubinstein and Elizabeth Arden?*

STL: I think it was my father. He was a wonderful merchant, and a great leader. He had no idea about this women's lib problem, but he believed in women, always. He believed that if you really were thoughtful and creative, you could accomplish anything. My husband taught me a great deal, too. None of the "men in my life" have had any qualms about believing in women. I think I've been very lucky in that.

BLDD: *Which of your previous careers was the most influential in developing your style as a designer?*

STL: It's a question of observing, all your life. I thought you might ask me today what my favorite hotels were. I remember them all vividly, from the time I was about six years old.

BLDD: *What* was *the first hotel you remember?*

STL: It was The Claypool Hotel, in Indianapolis, Indiana. We sang Christmas carols. I remember the French doors, fan lights, palms. It influenced very much how I did the indoor swimming pool in Rye—it is very Indianapolis.

BLDD: *Now, what is an Indianapolis lobby doing as a swimming pool in Rye, New York?*

STL: Something about the construction of the windows: they looked vaguely French and white lattice-y. And somehow, it's very romantic. I also remember the old Waldorf very well. The first great disillusionment in my life was, as a little girl, waking up early one morning to see what Peacock Alley really looked like. Of course, I never thought I'd be a hotel designer.

Sarah Tomerlin Lee

BLDD: *You've said that there may be better designers than you but there is none more romantic than you are. What you have in mind is for everybody to have a perfectly lovely time, no matter where they are. How do you try to accomplish that?*

STL: It came very strongly upon me when I was last in the Doral Country Club, in Florida. Everybody was there to have a lovely time. The spirit of the people was very exciting. I feel that's true here in New York when I see people walk through the Palace. I'm just delighted at their expressions. Recently we opened the most romantic hotel—the Parker Meridien. I notice people's delight as they come in and look around. It's amazing. I think if you give them a high ceiling and a beautiful vista, they do respond.

BLDD: *I have often thought that the first expression of your interest in design was what you did for Elizabeth Arden. Perhaps you can tell us about that.*

STL: If you are in merchandizing and retailing and advertising, you are always trying to come in on a different frequency. You try automatically to figure out what is different about your product. It seemed to me, with Arden's salons, that we should make a big feature of her red door. Now, Arden herself had painted her doors red. But I did the ad in the *New Yorker* with all those crazy red doors, to demonstrate her red-door salons all over this country and the world. We did booklets for peoples' appointments that looked like little red doors that opened. We just carried it right straight through. Almost everything I've ever learned I'm able to use somehow, even Latin.

BLDD: *How have you used the Latin?*

STL: One rainy afternoon, at what is now the bar at the Palace, we were peeling something off the ceiling, and we found a quotation from Seneca. I couldn't quite make it out, so I sent it down to my Latin teacher in Rappahannock, Virginia, Miss Willie Trueweathers. She sent me a perfect translation.

BLDD: *What was the quotation?*

STL: It was the same old business about "to your own self be true."

BLDD: *There are a number of phrases that you've added to our language. I'm thinking in particular of those you created as an advertising copywriter; tell us about them.*

STL: I had a lovely time in advertising. I analyzed women in bathing suits one time, when I had the Jantzen account. It seemed to me that the time when most people experience the greatest exposure is in trusting their bodies to about three-quarters of a yard of material. First I wrote a headline that said, "Just wear a Jantzen." Then I thought, that's miserable. I will say, "Just wear a smile—and a Jantzen." That headline ran for years. We did little smiles on lorgnettes for fashion shows. It's always nice if you can make something step out of a page, like the tiger in the tank. But I didn't think of that one.

BLDD: *Do you name the restaurants in the hotels that you design?*

STL: Yes, it's first of all a design clue. Hotels are trying to identify their restaurants as restaurants, not just as a place to eat in a hotel. So you give the restaurant all the individuality you can.

BLDD: *For the restaurant called Apley's in your recently opened hotel in Boston—named, I assume, for Marquand's Late George Apley—which came first, the name or the decor?*

STL: I usually work backward. I name things and then I try to do a "set" to fit the name. I think it's very helpful to have a name. Sometimes I'm given a name, and work that way. I did a restaurant once called The Lion's Share, because I thought it would appeal to men who might want a bigger martini or a bigger steak.

BLDD: *Of all your jobs, which has been the most gratifying?*

STL: This last one—the Parker Meridien—probably. It was a dream. Very few people in the world have a dream in three dimensions and have it come true.

BLDD: *You are referring to your most recent hotel, the Par-*

ker Meridien, on Fifty-seventh Street in Manhattan, that has an extraordinary atriumlike entranceway. Can you tell us something about that design?

STL: That design came about as a result of a handicap; the space on the Fifty-seventh Street side is only eighteen feet wide and 100 feet long. The real lobby is on Fifty-sixth street. It seemed to me, since it was a narrow space between two very tall buildings, that we should lift the ceiling as high as we could. I kept thinking about what I'd ever seen that was really a long narrow room. The most exciting one was the Trinity College Library in Dublin. And I remembered seeing Kenneth Clark, on television, going through the library in the Vatican. His comment to the audience was, "One wonders if man has ever had a really great idea in an enormous room." Then he turned and walked away, down this narrow room until he looked tiny. Well, I knew the Vatican library wasn't 100 feet long. I was also thinking about Palladio's Teatro Olimpico in Vicenza, which I had seen with my husband and the tremendous foreshortening effect of the way that was built, so that people seemed to become so small. But I realized that if you were walking down the long corridor at the Parker Meridien, someone might be coming the other way, so we couldn't do any tricks of perspective.

BLDD: *What did you do?*

STL: I just lifted the ceiling up fifty-four feet, six stories. There are enormous mirrors that reflect to infinity all along the walls. We have a beautiful marble floor, and a beautiful ceiling painted to look like mosaic inlay. We have it lighted during the day for daylight, then for moonlight after six o'clock.

BLDD: *How is color used in that lobby?*

STL: The colors in the front lobby are apricot, pale peach, beige and carnelian. The walls are white oak. It looks just fine. I was afraid at first that the columns were too orange, but we changed the lights and then it was all right.

114 BLDD: *From what I understand your son, Todd Lee, an*

architect based in Cambridge, helped to design that lobby space. Is Todd one of your secret weapons?

STL: He definitely is. When I have a real problem, I hop on a plane, or he flies down. He helped us a great deal with the canopies at the Palace. He also moved the front of the facade of the Sheraton Centre out on the sidewalk and gave us all those lovely places for breakfast and cocktails. He simplified the "Eskimo Modern" front that was on that hotel, so it's really handsome. One of the most charming things he has done is the quiet leafy oasis at the New York Hilton—in the discothèque which we called Sybil's. I wistfully said I wished we could have, somehow, the sound of water. I remember him saying in the first meeting, "Mother, if you want a torrent, you shall have it." And we have, flowing over the greenhouse.

BLDD: *I understand you have another son, a lawyer, who also assists you.*

STL: He is my legal advisor. And I'm proud of that.

BLDD: *Did you design the guest rooms in the Parker Meridien as well as the lobby and restaurant?*

STL: Yes, Warren McCurtain, our vice president, is really responsible for them, as he was for so much of the design in that unusual building.

BLDD: *Why don't we talk about hotel design in general for a moment: what—besides scale, obviously—makes designing a hotel different from designing an apartment? What's the difference between private and contract decorating?*

STL: It's a difference in how you service the person for whom you're designing. We never know who's coming for dinner. I have to just imagine what their tastes are. I think having been in advertising has helped me to analyze this.

BLDD: *How do you start a project? How do you determine what it's going to look like in terms of design, spirit, decor, furniture, color, lighting, cost?*

STL: Usually your costs are given to you. You know the job is going to be this many rooms, and this height, and whether it's going to be in the center of town, or out in the country. We're doing a hotel right now in St. Paul that was built in 1920, but has been closed for four years. Our job is in essence a revival.

BLDD: *Is it near the St. Paul Landmark Center? The purpose, I assume, of reopening the dormant hotel is to help revitalize the center of the city.*

STL: That's right. The hotel is part of that effort. We haven't yet started; we're still working on budgets and research.

BLDD: *Should a hotel designer—or any interior designer—use historical forms? Literally, how far do you go, and where do you do your research?*

STL: My attitude redesigning the Tarrytown Inn was very different from Rye. Although they are only ten miles apart, their design inspirations were one hundred years apart. Rye seemed to be very much a Victorian community, whereas Tarrytown was straight out-and-out eighteenth century. Great things in the American Revolution happened up and down the Hudson River. The people at the Sunnyside Restoration were very helpful to me with the Tarrytown project. For the Palace, we had two architectural historians who came along with the job. They were superb. We do a lot of research for many of our assignments. Not everything we do is historical, though.

BLDD: *Do you think that the current trend in architecture toward historic preservation and historicism itself has an enduring implication for interior design?*

STL: Oh, yes. I think we can cause things to bloom again, as they were.

BLDD: *How?*

STL: Colors and fabrics are part of it. I also discovered with the Palace project that there are still many really wonderful craftsmen. We found people who did absolutely marvelous plaster work. We found a man who could make a superb bronze stairway. The man who made the chandelier had been saving glorious crystals for years for The Great Chandelier. He also made the beautiful torchères. It was thrilling to work with these people.

BLDD: *The Palace is a fifty-one-story tower that rises above one of New York's celebrated brownstones designed by McKim, Mead & White. You are responsible for the restored section of what is referred to as the "Villard House" wing, in the hotel, as well as the public rooms within the rest of the Villard Houses. What were the most rewarding aspects of that assignment?*

STL: It was a dream. I couldn't believe it was real, because almost everything that you'd want to do, you *could* do.

BLDD: *How did you get the job?*

STL: I think Mr. Helmsley remembered by husband, who did the Park Lane Hotel, very well. He was very complimentary about Tom. Various people in the industry kept saying, "Write Mr. Helmsley, write him! He hasn't found a designer yet." I had never really made a presentation since the first job, so it was a hard letter to write.

BLDD: *Did you tell him of your background in historic preservation?*

STL: No, I don't think I mentioned that. I phoned him, and I heard him say it wasn't time. I was early. But the architect kept saying he wanted a designer right away. He didn't say he wanted us. And then I heard Mr. Helmsley's voice say, "Tell her it was a damn good letter." It does help to have been a writer. I went to see him with my samples. We went through them and he said, "I've seen that, I like that very much," or, "I didn't like that at all." Finally, he closed the book and said, "What have you ever done that's remotely like what I have in mind for the Palace?" "Nothing," I said. "Nor has anyone else." And he said, "Well, I guess *you'd* better do it." I think everybody else was probably trying too hard to get the job.

BLDD: *I assume that one of the things you were striving for there was a kind of old-world elegance.*

STL: Those rooms really couldn't be changed; they just had to be waked up. I remember going to Williamsburg the first time, when I was in college. They told me that the reason the Rockefellers put their money in Williamsburg rather than in some more historic city—Boston, Philadelphia—was because it was

Sarah Tomerlin Lee
Woodcliff Lake Hilton Inn
Woodcliff Lake, New Jersey
1980

115

a sleeping beauty. They could kiss it and it would come to life. You can't do that in New York, they say. Well, this has been true of the Villard Houses.

BLDD: *What goals were you striving for in the Palace—and do you think you managed to achieve them?*

STL: Not entirely. I wish there were more flow of traffic, more open vistas. We had to respect the original walls; after all it was built as a private house. But we did discover some wonderful things. There's great elegance there, which people today are hungry for. I think the new ballroom is extremely pretty. I really love that oval room. The very fact that we could design a small ballroom that wasn't divided, and could never house a convention meeting, was wonderful.

BLDD: *What's the maximum capacity of the room?*

STL: It's 230 people. It has lovely historic murals and a carpet that we had woven in England.

BLDD: *Why "The Palace"? How have you reinforced the name "Palace" in your design?*

STL: At first I was embarrassed by the name. It seemed so pretentious, but as I look at it and see it now, polished and shining, I think it *is* a palace. There's so much marble and inlaid mosaic; the floors are all inlaid. It was made much more beautiful by the Whitelaw Reid family, when Reid was Ambassador to Great Britain. The final flourish was put on it when the Prince of Wales came here for a big party at Christmastime in about 1901. That's when they pulled out every stop and had those beautiful fireplaces made by St. Gaudens. The fireplace with fountains is pretty spectacular. If you're the designer, all you should do in a place like the Palace, I think, is respect the treasure.

BLDD: *Well, you have done that. How do you feel, on the other hand, about waking up and knowing that you're in a Sheraton or a Hilton? Or do you think that hotel rooms should be anonymous?*

STL: I think you should always know where you are when you wake up. I don't mean that you should have a picture of Fifth Avenue staring at you. But it's wonderful if you can somehow sense that you are in the East or in the South. If everything is the same, it's a miserable trip. Part of the pleasure of travel is to find characteristics of the place where you are.

BLDD: *In that sense, your view differs from several other hotel designers. How do you compare your view with theirs?*

STL: I understand why big hotel chains want to superimpose patterns of taste—it's a multiple order. I don't decry what they have done. I have great respect for the cleanliness, the way furnishings last, and the way they defy vandalism. It's just that I would like to lift everybody's taste a little.

BLDD: *What should be the standard of good design in a hotel? Should it be conservative, should it be a little bit avant-garde?*

STL: It's hard. We can be very avant-garde in a suite. We did a suite at the New York Hilton that rents for $1,700 a night. When we were trying to have a fund-raising party in that suite for the restoration of rooms in City Hall, there were only two nights in the year that it was free. Can you believe it?

BLDD: *Hardly. Who rents those rooms?*

STL: Big corporations and governments and rich people. They love it. There are two maid's rooms, and we had to have a security room. When the Democratic Convention was here I realized that seven presidential candidates were sleeping in our guest rooms across the city. I was as proud as I could be.

BLDD: *In contrast to your work at the Palace are the country inns that you've done. How do you feel about the design of country inns?*

STL: They're a great opportunity, I think, because they can be sweet. You can relax, and do lovely doorways, and have terraces planted with flowers. In Tarrytown, we moved the dining room wall out overlooking the rose garden, and it's just lovely now. In Rye, there is a beautiful pool outside, and we planted a strawberry walk, and a violet patch. If you take just a little bit more trouble to make everybody have a wonderful time, they do.

BLDD: *I'm still amazed at the cost of that hotel room that you*

Sarah Tomerlin Lee
Rendering for Sheraton Centre
renovation
New York, N.Y.
completed 1980

just mentioned. I assume a lot of design, particularly in hotels, takes its shape and form from statistics—for example, the percentage of travelers who are male, the cost of electricity, and so on. How do you make a room "traveler-proof"?

STL: We saved two million dollars in the New York Hilton by changing, unhappily, to fluorescent lights in the corridors. Corridor lights never go out. We use heavy vinyls that look very elegant and don't tear or mar. We know there will be a certain loss. If you judged by the average traveler, you wouldn't think much of the human race. I try not to think about this. For instance, you must have pictures larger than a suitcase. You must be careful about the bedspread: it must be too bulky to put it in a garment bag. That's quite shocking, isn't it?

BLDD: *Is that why hotel hangers have been locked into place so that you can't even get your clothes on them while you're there?*

STL: That's right. Now, some hotel people say, "Take it." I once designed a little shop in a new hotel in Canada called Take It All Home—But Pay For It. I had an illustration of a very chic lady with a great big hotel on her back. The shop sold special plates and special towels which we had designed. It was quite a success. In the guest rooms that we just finished at the Parker Meridien, there is a great big terry robe on every bed, folded as though you should take it. This is true at the Palace, too. But there's a little note saying that if you want to take it, it will be on your bill. It's not rude, or they wouldn't have put it there. At the same time, they put out all sorts of little goodies in the bathroom—the shower cap, the soap, the sewing box—that they hope you will take. They expect that.

BLDD: *It seems to me that in the past five years or so, hotel executives have discovered that there are women travelers: everything isn't brown anymore.*

STL: That was a terrible problem when I started. It was as though we were supposed to do the insides of cigar boxes. They'd say that eighty percent of the travelers were men. But before my time, Hilton had the idea that there were some *women* executives. They did a floor called Lady Hilton. And after just a few months, they discovered that men were coming in asking for Lady Hilton rooms, because—I suppose—they were more like home. Those rooms had prettier curtains and softer chairs. They were almost totally occupied by men, who loved them. I think that men's idea of what is acceptable has changed. Everybody wants more color. It's a softer approach, and they don't feel it's unmasculine to like something that's beautiful.

BLDD: *Aside from color and comfort and looking more like home, there are certain things that women who travel alone must bear in mind when they check into a hotel. For example, is the room close to an elevator, or are the corridors well lit. Do you deal with that in your hotel design?*

STL: Not for women in particular; we must do those things for everybody now. We must have well-lit corridors, and we must have all kinds of protection. There have been great advances in locks—cards instead of keys, etc.

BLDD: *By and large, I guess, it's men who are making the decisions whether to accept or reject your designs. How do you get along with all these men?*

STL: There's no problem at all, once they believe in you. They now know that the palette has changed completely. Other designers have helped produce that change, too. We're deep into a wisteria, orchid, pale green and blue cycle. We're out of the brown, and that strong blue and white and brown and white stage. Now everything is much softer, with lots of lovely pale chintzes and patterned rugs. It's a big change.

BLDD: *You design a lot of rugs for your jobs yourself. For what location did you design that beautiful oriental patterned rug that we have here?*

STL: It is for the Rainier's dining room in the Sheraton Centre in New York. It is an oriental pattern, as you say, but we changed the colors and the scale.

117

118

Sarah Tomerlin Lee
"Le Patio"
Parker Meridien Hotel
New York, N.Y.
1981

BLDD: *What inspired the design for that rug, for example?*
STL: It just happened to be the rug in my living room!
BLDD: *Until ten years ago you had never designed a public space—but had you designed your own private space?*
STL: No, never; I couldn't and be Tom Lee's wife. He wanted to please me, but he really chose everything himself. And he knew a lot more about it than I did. I just loved what he did.
BLDD: *How involved are your clients in the design process?*
STL: Often, if you're trying to do something innovative, you have to explain it to them to lead them into it. It's the same if you're selling an advertising campaign. We show them the furniture that we want. Frequently they want to sit in the chairs, especially if it's a cocktail lounge. They'll sit back and they'll say, "Is this a two-martini chair?"
BLDD: *What's a two-martini chair?*
STL: It has to be big enough and supportive enough.
BLDD: *How in the world did you manage to convince a first-time developer in New York to have a six-story lobby?*
STL: I talked to him about his competition. I said, "You are starting out in this field, you are facing the great giants who have been here fifty years ahead of you. There's very little press left, so publicity must be word of mouth. The hotel must be a gift to the city of New York, a romantic 'folie,' so people will go to Fifty-sixth Street between Sixth and Seventh avenues to see it. That's the greatest thing I can do for you. And I'd say it'll cost you quite a lot. But I think that we'll see quickly how this works. Very soon, people will say, 'Oh, have you been there?'" I was a copywriter at Bonwit Teller, in 1938, during the period of "the Smart Woman's Angle." The vice president, Sara Pennoyu, and my husband, Tom Lee, who was the display director, and some brilliant buyers developed patterns in merchandising that were later used by Lord & Taylor and other stores. It was a very innovative period. We broke a lot of rules. We had everybody thrilled about that store. And we didn't want to do what anybody else did.
BLDD: *And you still don't...*

STL: No, I don't. I think that was fine training for me. Anyway, I told Mr. Parker that I felt this was the way he should approach the hotel. It was on a very strangely shaped property—what had been the old Great Northern Hotel. The block seemed a bit shabby to me. So we had to do something magnificent.
BLDD: *Are you pleased with the results?*
STL: Yes, I really am. I must say we all were very inspired at this challenge.
BLDD: *You mentioned earlier that since your first job, you've never applied for one, other than the letter to Mr. Helmsley about the Palace. How do you get your clients?*
STL: The hotel world is very small. They tell each other everything. They show each other everything. They sell you even to their competitors. Isn't that peculiar?
BLDD: *It's generous.*
STL: It is.
BLDD: *You mentioned the classic hotels before. Won't you describe some recent ones that meet your standards of character and quality?*
STL: I love the Berkshire Place, which just opened. I think it's delicious, elegant and romantic. It's done by Roland N. Jutras. I am thrilled by the cocktail lounge at the Hyatt over Forty-second Street. They took a great opportunity and made a wonderful spot.
BLDD: *What makes it so wonderful—the lighting? the decor?*
STL: It's the realization of the space: it just hangs in the air over that busy street. Hotel design has largely become theater, entertainment. We're really quite theatrical without, I hope, being cheap. We try to set a stage for people at great moments in their lives.
BLDD: *What's the difference between a decorator and a designer, and which one are you?*
STL: I hope I'm a designer. Decorators change the chintz.
BLDD: *And what do designers do?*
STL: They might change the door, or the window. We like to

approach jobs very architecturally. It isn't always possible, because we do so many old buildings over. That's a great challenge. It's sometimes very difficult.

BLDD: *You've said, on numerous occasions in fact, that every handicap is a challenge. Can you tell us of some of these handicaps that you've turned to your advantage?*

STL: One was that long, narrow space at the Parker Meridien. We have also been working to bring the Roosevelt Hotel back to where it used to be when I was a young girl visiting New York. There are some beautiful public spaces there but as time went by, people used them for offices and walled things up. We have a beautiful big oval reception tea room there now, and a lobby cocktail lounge that looks like a fine library. And we have wonderful paintings. We've torn down a lot of fake walls and found lovely paneling. The discovery of what was once there is very exciting to me.

BLDD: *Sixteen years ago, soon after you became the editor of* House Beautiful, *an issue came out in which you wrote, "Because we feel that conformity is a deadly blanket over the land, we've dedicated this entire issue to the individualist." You decided in that issue to salute those who step beyond conformity. "Individualism," you said, "once the glorious prerogative of wealth, fame and beauty, is now the reward of the aware." Do you still feel this way? How have you translated that philosophy into your design work?*

STL: I just determinedly don't do what I've ever done before. I also don't do anything that anybody else ever did, if I know it. We're not struggling to be outrageous and outlandish, but we try not to have a mark of ourselves on what we do. Each place should be a different interpretation of the best we can do.

BLDD: *Would you like your work to be identified as a job by Sarah Tomerlin Lee?*

STL: I just want people to think it's beautiful. This is very egotistical, I suppose, but I would love them to say, "It's so beautiful that the Lee organization must have designed it."

120

Sarah Tomerlin Lee
"The Hunt Bar"
Helmsley Palace
New York, N.Y.
1980

122

Sarah Tomerlin Lee
"The Gold Room"
Helmsley Palace
New York, N.Y.
1980

Sarah Tomerlin Lee
"The Madison Room"
Helmsley Palace
New York, N.Y.
1980

Sarah Tomerlin Lee
Doorway detail
Rye Town Hilton Inn
Port Chester, New York
1973

Sarah Tomerlin Lee
Bedrooms
Rye Town Hilton Inn
Port Chester, New York
1973

126

Sarah Tomerlin Lee
Lobby
Parker Meridien Hotel
New York, N.Y.
1981

Sarah Tomerlin Lee
Arcade and 57th Street entrance
Parker Meridien Hotel
1981

BLDD: *Warren Platner says he's just about the only architect who really believes that a building's design comes from within. Perhaps you can tell us what that really means, and how your view differs from that of other people?*

WP: I think that most people who design buildings or even do interior work in buildings think of the building as a package—an object in the landscape or in the city. They conceive of it that way, and then they fit the space inside that envelope.

BLDD: *How do you do it?*

WP: I try to think of how the space in a building will be used. I could give a specific example: several years ago we did a public library building, the Kent Memorial Library in Suffield, Connecticut. It was one of the first jobs we did. In that building, the entire structure, even its relation to the site, and so on, develops from a concept of what the building should be inside. There is nothing imposed from conceiving first what the outside of the building should be and then adapting the interior needs to it. The first step I took in thinking about that building was trying to conceive of what would be the best atmosphere, the best character, for a small town public library building. In other words, where would you like to go to browse for books, or perhaps to sit down and read?

BLDD: *How innovative can you be in designing a library? There are books and there are stacks and there are lights and desks and chairs. What did you do?*

WP: My thought was that you could have an intimate character and a small-scale interior. If you thought of it as your library at home, it would be a small room lined with books, with some comfortable furniture and maybe a fireplace. And it would have an intimate atmosphere. It would be cozy. It would be warm in esthetic character because there'd be books all around the walls. Forget public buildings and institutions like libraries, and think about where you would like to be if you were looking for a book or reading, or doing your homework from school.

128 BLDD: *Where would you like to be?*

WP: I thought that the best thing would be to have small-scale spaces with intimate character. But a public building still has to have a considerable amount of space in it.

BLDD: *How do you create an intimate space within that kind of environment?*

WP: We had to have many spaces in the building. We wanted intimate spaces and places for books. We thought of how to organize those spaces in such a way that you wouldn't enter the building and find yourself in a maze. You would want to walk in and clearly understand where things are and what spaces there are and how to find your way around. The first thing that we did with that concept was to think of it as a doughnut. We made many individual, intimate spaces and arranged them around an opening in the middle of the building, a garden court, a very glassy transparent space. Immediately, as you enter, you can see all the other spaces across that court and you can understand the building. So this building started out with a concept of what the character and the scale and the atmosphere of the space should be. That first concept was obviously an interior concept: how are you going to use the building? What is the plan derived from that?

BLDD: *A fundamental decision, of course: where did you place the books?*

WP: We put the books around the walls of the spaces, as you would if it were your library at home.

BLDD: *In contrast to a usual open shelf and stack library that we're familiar with?*

WP: Usually libraries have reading rooms where you do your reading, and then they have stacks where the books are stored, as if they're in a book warehouse. Our building is roughly square in plan. It has a square opening in the middle, which is an outdoor garden court with a fountain and a tree and hedges and flowers and so on. The spaces around that court are relatively small. Some of them are larger than you would have in your house, and some of them are perhaps as large as a large residential library. They all either look in on

Warren Platner

the garden court, or out the other side to the town green.

BLDD: *You and your forty associates have your practice in New Haven. One of the things you pride yourselves on is the unusually broad range of services that you offer, including everything from building design to furnishings to lighting to landscape design. How does that all work? Are there specialists among the forty?*

WP: Not really. Almost everyone in my firm is trained as an architect. I try to develop versatility in the people who work with me as well as in myself. My feeling is that as far as education goes, an architectural education is a very thorough one and encompasses virtually every aspect of the plastic arts, as well as aspects of engineering and many other disciplines. Architects can, therefore, do almost any design task they wish, if they care enough about what they're doing.

BLDD: *With forty such versatile associates, how many jobs can you take on at any given time?*

WP: We limit ourselves in the number of projects that we take, for several reasons. One is that I don't wish to be an administrator; I don't wish to be an organizer; I don't wish to be just a salesman. I am interested in doing the work myself.

BLDD: *How many jobs are you all working on now?*

WP: I can handle somewhere between eight and fifteen jobs at any given time.

BLDD: *That's quite a range. Can you manage to involve yourself in each of these projects when you have fifteen?*

WP: Yes. It depends, of course. When I say fifteen projects, they're in various phases. Some may be in the final stage of construction, others may just be starting out in concept. The amount of attention required varies with the stage and nature of the project. We're doing some very small projects presently and some very large ones. I don't wish to suggest that small projects aren't as complicated as large ones—they are. But large ones are complex because they can really be many different projects all put together as one.

BLDD: *What's the largest and the smallest, so that we get some idea of the range of your work.*

WP: Currently, our largest project is a corporate headquarters and speculative office building for Sea Containers, on the Thames, in the center of London. It is about three-quarters of a million square feet. It's T-shaped and seventeen stories high. It's about a city block long. An acre for instance has 44,000 square feet in it. So you can relate three-quarters of a million to that.

BLDD: *And what's a smaller job that your office is currently involved in?*

WP: At the moment we're designing plumbing fixtures for one of the largest plumbing fixture manufacturers in the world. We are designing a bidet, a water closet, a bathtub and a lavatory. They're not a building, or an interior; in some ways it's a simpler project than a large one like the building in London. Especially since within many of our projects, such as the Sea Container building, we've designed all the furniture—not the chairs, but all the desks and so on—as part of the project.

BLDD: *You've often said that architecture is not a personal expression like painting, sculpture and the other arts; and that the architect is here to serve others' needs, not to express himself. That's not a very widely shared view, is it?*

WP: That's right. If I'm a painter, I'm expressing myself in my medium. If I'm a sculptor, it's the same thing. I can comment on life, on the world, on mores, on events, on whatever I want. I can paint a landscape which simply shows you something that I saw. But I also have the liberty, because it is a personal expression, of limiting myself to how *I* feel about things. I don't think that's what an architect or designer should be doing. His task is to serve peoples' needs, and he should not be imposing his psychological views, and so on, on other people. He should figure out what they should have, and to do so he has to think of things from their point of view rather than from his own.

BLDD: *At what stage in the design process does the client become involved?*

129

WP: From the beginning.

BLDD: *And how* involved *is involved?*

WP: I think the best client is the most interested one. An apathetic client—a client who's too busy to pay attention to his project—is a very poor client, indeed. I like a client who cares. If he's fascinated by it, he's going to react to what is presented to him as ways of resolving his needs, and he's going to contribute to the project. I like that. I don't care where the ideas come from. They don't have to come from me, they don't have to come from other people in my organization. As long as the ideas come.

BLDD: *You set up your own practice a little less than fifteen years ago. Before that you worked with Raymond Loewy, Eero Saarinen, then the inheritors of the Saarinen office, and very briefly, for I. M. Pei.*

WP: Yes, and for Yamasaki, also. I helped a lot of people along with their careers before I started my own practice.

BLDD: *Did any of them have the opportunity to help you? What, in that range of experience, has helped make you the kind of versatile designer that you are?*

WP: My experience with Raymond Loewy Associates showed me that it could be fascinating and worthwhile to pay attention to a very simple object. Where does architecture end? Where does space end? The objects in space modify the space and have a lot to do with the success of it. So the success of the object is important, too. It was brought home to me in a very clear way that I could design all those things, and make them happen. I think the most important thing I learned from Eero Saarinen was that hard work is really very worthwhile. He was an extremely hard-working person. He really *lived* architecture all the time. His work was his life. And mine has become the same way.

BLDD: *Was it while you were with Saarinen that you became particularly interested in the interiors of buildings and the new frontiers of technology, as well?*

130 WP: Yes. I discovered that in a way we were slighting the

Warren Platner
Georg Jensen Design Center
1968

attention to the interior architecture. We were designing buildings as if their systems were the most important thing. And actually, to be very specific, it came about in a rather obvious manner. One of the things that an architect does is to determine all the materials of a building. And he usually determines the colors that the materials are painted. One of the first experiences I had when I was with what was then Saarinen and Saarinen was to make the color selections for a complex of buildings at Drake University.

There was a student union and dormitories and so on. They were very simple buildings and there was a lot of paint to go on the walls and ceilings. We were the architects for the project, but it was assumed that some other organization would be selecting the furniture and so on. And I said, "How can I pick colors? How can you do part of a scheme? If I do part of a scheme, then whoever is going to complete the scheme is stuck with my decisions, and my decisions weren't made with the benefit of knowing how they would work with the next person's. The next person wasn't free to make the decisions, since I had made them." So I said that if we were going to do the buildings we ought to do all the interiors of the buildings. We ought to conceive of the building from the inside out. And that's how I became so interested in interiors. It was simply a matter of being faced with decisions I didn't believe I could make under the circumstances.

BLDD: *How soon after that was the first Warren Platner chair created?*

WP: The first furniture design that I did completely on my own was started in about 1960. That was the wire furniture for Knoll, and it went on the market about five years later, around 1965.

BLDD: *You're one of the people who claims to have known early on the direction of your life. Was there any particular circumstance or individual that helped direct your interest?*

WP: When I was a boy I used to like to make things with my hands. Nothing very significant, bird houses and things like

that. And I was very interested in materials. I thought of flowers as a material, and I used to like to arrange flowers because I thought of them as sculpture. If you put these over there and these here, you can make something of it. If you think about architecture and interior design, it's a similar thing. You have this object and that object and this material and that material, and then you have this structure. Flowers have structure, too. And that, I think, is the genesis of how I became interested in architecture.

BLDD: *One of the things your firm prides itself on is its role in developing original systems. Perhaps you can tell us about some of them.*

WP: About fifteen years ago, here in New York, we did a project called the Jensen Design Center. The space, and the design, don't exist any more because the company has since gone out of business. That very small project—about 12,000 square feet—had in it many things we conceived of which are now fairly ubiquitous in the architecture and design world. One of our tasks was to put George Jensen on the map as a factor in furniture and lighting and fabrics and to attract the attention of other designers and architects. And one way that we conceived of doing that was to do things that were entirely fresh in the design of the center.

BLDD: *I suspect that's the intent of most good designers. But what did you do that was fresh?*

WP: We reinvented what is a very popular thing today, the trompe l'oeil wall, where you create the effect of three-dimensional space, form, architecture, on a flat plane. We did that there in several ways. The most unusual was by projection. Opposite the entrance, when you came off the elevators, we had a very large white wall. The space was not dark, but it was relatively dimly lit. And we projected images of objects and places and buildings and interiors on that wall. It was like facing a billboard when you came off the elevators.

BLDD: *Had that technique not been done widely in recent times?*

WP: Not using projection. Almost anything one does that doesn't involve new technology has been done in some way before. It's how you do it that makes it innovative. We also did large photographic blow-ups, to give the effect of a forest out the window. So we had two methods by which we created a false or make-believe sense of three-dimensional space and form.

BLDD: *What else did you introduce in the Jensen Design Center?*

WP: For the first time anywhere, I think, we used theatrical lighting effects to create a special lighting which was decorative in itself, rather than just lighting the floor, or the objects, or the whole space.

Theater designers had been doing this for a long time, but nobody had done it in interior design or architecture. That has also become very popular today. Another thing we did was use all-glass detailing for our partitions. The partitions were pieces of glass from floor to ceiling and they were braced by other pieces of glass at right angles to the main pieces of glass. We used silicone-filled joints, and patch hardware, and all those things that are ubiquitous today.

BLDD: *Can you cite some examples of where that glass partitioning has since been used?*

WP: In our next project, we put it on the exterior of a building. And in the Prospect Center in Princeton, we encased the whole building in all-glass detail. It's a lovely effect. It creates a very crystalline result. An example that everyone might know is the National Airlines Terminal at Kennedy Airport.

BLDD: *I suspect there must have been uses of glass other than yours at that time, and, I guess, less and less use of glass today, because of energy consciousness. How would you use that glass now? Would it have to be tinted?*

WP: Not necessarily. You could make a double wall of glass. There are many things you can do.

BLDD: *But if cost were a factor?*

WP: It's simply using glass structurally instead of introducing 131 another material, such as masonry or wood or metal, to support the glass. It's a very simple concept, one that architects take quite for granted today. And it has not been abandoned by any means: it's very popular right now for glazing exteriors of buildings. And, of course, it's used for interiors.

BLDD: *One of your interiors was one of the most widely talked about restaurants of the 1970s—Windows on the World, on top of the World Trade Center in New York. I think it was Paul Goldberger, the architecture critic of the* New York Times, *who said that your style might be called "sensuous modernism." I think what he means is the use of lush, rich materials that have a clean line. Would that be an accurate or a fair description?*

WP: It's reasonable. If I were to describe Windows on the World, I would have to say that our first thought there was to make people comfortable. When you go out to dine, it's a very special occasion. You're not just going out to eat. When you go to a restaurant, you're looking for an effect that you cannot get at home.

BLDD: *Was your priority to innovate, or to create a comfortable setting?*

WP: A comfortable setting, number one. Entertainment, number two. When you go to a place like Windows on the World, there's a view, of course, and you might think that everyone would wish to sit as close to the windows as possible, and they would think they had a second-rate table if they couldn't. So one of the tasks at Windows on the World was to make every table the best in the house.

BLDD: *How do you give everybody a slice of the view in a limited space?*

WP: It's not only a slice of the view. Some people have a better view than others, so you give the others compensating things.

BLDD: *For example, there are niches there. I assume that farther from the window, the environments become more decorative.*

WP: And more intimate. When people go out to dine, they're really looking for what I call "convivial intimacy." You wouldn't go to a restaurant if there were nobody else there. People don't like empty restaurants. You really want the conviviality of a lot of other people. But when you sit down at your table and survey the scene and so on, you forget all those other people and it becomes an intimate occasion. So in a large dining room, those little alcoves are really in a way the best place to sit, because they're the most intimate of the spaces. And you still have a view, even though you're farthest away from the windows. It's one example of how you might go about trying to make people especially comfortable. By comfort I mean many different things; not just physical comfort, but psychological comfort, too.

BLDD: *Among the things that you did there was to place people on different levels so that they could have a part of that view, weather permitting. And you made fashionable, as well, the idea of a pavilion within a restaurant. Did you ever expect the restaurant to be the popular success that it was?*

WP: That had to be my goal from the start. Whenever I embark on anything, I look at it from the standpoint that it must be as great a success as I can make it. And that was true with Windows on the World. When Guy Tozzoli, the director of the World Trade Center, first came to me, he said, "We would like to have the finest business luncheon club in the city, within our projected budget. But we can't afford to have a place that simply serves lunch. So it will have to be a public restaurant at night. A commercial operation. And you're going to have a very hard time getting people to come. Because there's nobody down in this section of New York at night. There are no stores, no theaters, no night life. And people are going to have to make that trip all the way down here."

BLDD: *There had already been a great deal of negative criticism of the buildings themselves.*

WP: Yes, the World Trade Center was a dirty word. People didn't like it because the press, and the politicians, had used the Port Authority and the World Trade Center as a whipping boy for about fifteen years while it was being planned and constructed. We were very much aware of that when we started the project. It was a personal objective to make it as successful as possible. And by successful, I mean popular. I was not interested in telling people about how Warren Platner conceives of a restaurant; I was interested in making a place where people would really wish to be. But there was also the charge from the client that, by god, it had better be successful, because people aren't just going to happen in here, they're going to have to come on purpose.

BLDD: *Why don't you tell us about some of the lush and sensuous materials that you used there to lure them downtown?*

WP: We really laid it on. Perhaps the best example is the men's toilet room. It has a silk ceiling and pink marble and a lot of mirrors and a lot of lights. That was very deliberate. The entire experience of going to dine at Windows on the World was the important thing, as I conceived it. Any part of that is part of the experience. The best advertising for any restaurant is word-of-mouth. If people go away saying nice things about it, it doesn't matter what aspect they're talking about.

BLDD: *How about the food and service?*

WP: That's part of it too. But I would like to illustrate this point by telling you a little story. Usually the women's powder room gets a lot of attention in a fancy place like that, but the men's room is rather perfunctorily treated. We decided not to do that in this case. About two weeks after Windows on the World opened, I was in Kansas City. I had an appointment with a friend of mine out there, the president of Hall's Store. I went into his reception room, and there wasn't anyone at the reception desk, so I walked over to his office. His door was open and he was on the telephone. So I stood outside the door for a minute, waiting for him to finish his conversation. A man came up to me and said, "May I help you?" I said, "Oh, no thank you, I'm just waiting for Jack to finish his telephone conversation." And he said, "Oh, you must be Warren Platner. That toilet room!" In Kansas City, two weeks after it opened!

BLDD: *They also know you for your valentines in Kansas City. You ended up doing a restaurant there that was sort of a valentine to the city, and not accidentally.*

WP: It wasn't consciously a valentine, but our client was Hallmark, the greeting card company. There's a certain esthetic implied there—very pretty, cute things. The intent was to do something very special for them. There's no reason why Kansas City shouldn't have a particular character and style and design just the way Windows on the World has its own character and design. When I start a project, I'm always looking for the hook to hang it on. Where does the conception come from? And thinking of Crown Center, which was the name of the group of buildings, and of the clients and their principal business—greeting cards—I did something that's like a lace valentine. It was described that way by somebody else; I didn't describe it that way. But it's apt—it's a very pretty, lacy thing.

BLDD: *You obviously have a very singular point of view that you've had the opportunity to express in a wide range of fields. I find it especially interesting that you've worked in collaboration with so many distinguished architects, each of whom has also had a very singular point of view. I'm thinking of Roche/Dinkeloo at the Ford Foundation, Edward Larrabee Barnes at the Crown Center, and I. M. Pei and Partners, with whom you're currently involved in a hotel project in Singapore. How does that all work out—who's ego is subsumed, and at what point in the process?*

WP: Many of our projects come to us through other architects. In fact, the Singapore project came to us from I. M. Pei himself. He called me up and explained the project and their need, and asked if we would be interested in working with them. I like to think that architects appreciate us more than anyone else. They should. Architects know their field better than anyone else. If we are very good at what we do, we should be most

133

Warren Platner
Water Tower Place
Chicago, Illinois
1977

Warren Platner
Prospect Center
Princeton University
Princeton, New Jersey
1970

appreciated by other architects.

BLDD: *And what do you offer that's so unusual that an architect would go to you to create a part of his design—the interiors, the furniture, the lighting?*

WP: Interior design, done well, is much more difficult than doing the building itself. It means dealing not with systems or structures of building, but dealing with people, and what makes them psychologically comfortable—what are they going to do in the space, how are they going to live in it, work in it, and so on. Those things are intangible and difficult to cope with. And time consuming—there's a great deal of detail involved. Architects find it much more rewarding to devote energy to building large structures; there's an idea out there that anybody's wife can do the interiors, but a building is much too complicated for anybody but an architect to handle. Therefore, architects get their way more easily when they're dealing with building structures. They're easier to do, and they go up faster. They're bigger monuments, they count more on the horizon, people notice them more. And I believe that architects shy away from really caring very much about interior work because it is so difficult to do. Their egos are stroked better the other way. They get much more prominence.

BLDD: *I was under the impression that there were many architects who not only wanted but insisted on doing the interior, so that in some way it would reflect their intent in terms of the larger design.*

WP: Some do. But I have to point out that we're doing the most important interiors in I. M. Pei's project in Singapore, at his request.

BLDD: *One of the largest projects that you've worked on was Water Tower Place, in Chicago. It's a whole city block, seventy stories high, what you might call an instant landmark. More people meet at the interior of that central elevator shaft than most any other place in Chicago. What specific design problems did such a project present to you?*

134   WP: Water Tower Place has no exterior space to speak of. The

building goes from sidewalk to sidewalk and sidewalk to sidewalk for the entire block. And it's packed with many different functions. There are fifty stories of apartments, there's a twenty-story hotel, an office building, one of the largest shopping centers in the world, four theaters, a parking garage, and other things within the building.

BLDD: *How would you describe the shape of that space?*

WP: It's not a complex of buildings; it's all one big block of building structure. And when you think about all of that in one city block, you realize that there's very limited street frontage for any one of the functions within the building. The most difficult aspect was that our clients were planning to build a shopping mall of some hundred to hundred-fifty stores, and virtually all of that was going to be tucked out of sight vertically within the building. Obviously, you have to have street frontage to approach your hotel, and, you have to have street frontage to approach the apartments. There were also two big department stores that needed some street frontage. There was no way to do a shopping mall in the conventional sense, so it could be seen from the street. As a matter of fact, the mall starts two levels above the street. We had to make an entrance so compelling, so inviting, and so dramatic, that you couldn't fail to want to go up there and check it out.

BLDD: *Almost like an English garden, you've managed to lure people up, level after level.*

WP: Our concept was, in effect, to extend the street and the sidewalk, but as a tropical garden—sort of as a tropical Villa d'Este or Tivoli—to lead you up to where the mall begins. Our original concept for that portion of the building started with that idea of how to pull people up there. It's a long way, both vertically and horizontally, up escalators. (There are stairs, also, because there have to be, by law.) It's a long way from where you enter to where you reach the top. We arranged that space and the elements in it to make the distance from bottom to top seem much shorter than it was. One way we did this, which I think most people don't realize, was to use false per-

spective. The escalators diverge as they go up; they're not parallel to each other. In perspective, parallel lines converge on a point in the distance, so if you spread the lines apart, it makes the distance seem closer to you. Of course, when you come out of the mall, it's the reverse. But we've had you by then!

BLDD: *One of the most neglected areas of design is the office, though many of us spend most of our time there. What are the prospects for a more humane use of office space?*

WP: You're asking me about the future. I'm so taken up with today and living life as it is that I'm not really very concerned about the future. That's going to be somebody else's task, not mine.

BLDD: *How about the here and now? You're engaged, for example, in a very large project in Singapore. What are you going to do to make the lives of those occupants more enjoyable while at work?*

WP: I care very much about the quality of what we do; I don't care about the quantity of what we do. I care about every detail of what we're concerned with. And I think that is the answer to what makes spaces livable, workable—spaces that enrich one's life, that make one feel comfortable. All these things should be considered when the spaces in buildings are determined. Unfortunately, I think the trend in my profession is against exactly that. Architectural firms are getting larger and larger, and there is a whole new profession of interior design firms that aren't architectural at all. I don't think it's a good idea to divide the two. I think it's an abdication of the architect's responsibility.

BLDD: *How do you make the distinction between an interior designer and an interior decorator?*

WP: I'm both. And I'm an architect.

BLDD: *Do you think all interior designers should be architecturally trained?*

WP: Yes, I do. I think that there are many disciplines that they lack if they don't have an architectural education.

BLDD: *And you can't see any room for any other kind of training?*

WP: Oh, absolutely. Thomas Jefferson was an architect. He didn't study architecture. I don't believe that there is any one rule about how one comes to one's ability to do things. I just think that it is unfortunate that as architectural and design firms became larger and larger and larger the people who are best in those firms do not limit their work. They're spread so thin that they cannot really do a quality job anymore.

BLDD: *Often a necessity, because they've got to maintain the office.*

WP: One way out is to design systems. But I think systems are anti-people. People don't like systems. I travel by air a lot. I hate flying because I hate the way I'm treated by the airlines. Why do I hate the way I'm treated by the airlines? Because I'm put into their system.

BLDD: *Have you ever designed the interior of an airline?*

WP: No, I haven't. I'd like to.

BLDD: *How do you live? What's your Warren Platner house like?*

WP: My own house is formal. By "formal" I mean it's not casual. It's not one space sliding into another. It has distinct rooms and spaces in it. Definite rooms. On the other hand, I like to lie on the floor. I'm very dressed up today; usually I wear some old Levis and a work shirt. I like to live informally in formal spaces. But you have to understand what I mean by formal.

BLDD: *You've said that you were forty before you knew what you were doing. What were you doing until that time?*

WP: Pretending I knew what I was doing.

BLDD: *How did you get away with it?*

WP: Fortunately—or unfortunately—many people don't make the distinction between what is well done and what isn't well done. So you can easily get away with telling people you're good, even though you know you aren't.

Warren Platner
Georg Jensen Design Center
1968

Warren Platner's living room
1971

Following page:
Warren Platner
Wire furniture
1965

141

Warren Platner
Kent Memorial Library
Suffield, Connecticut
1972

Next page:
Warren Platner
Dining room
Windows on the World
New York, N.Y.
1975

BLDD: *John Saladino once studied painting at Yale University—so it's not surprising that he describes his interiors as walk-in paintings. I wonder if you can tell us, John, what that unusual and fascinating description really means. What do the two have in common?*

JS: I don't regard interior design as an applied art, but as a fine art. We look upon the interior as participating in art; it's art that you live in, rather than art that you look at.

BLDD: *How do you make a still life livable? What place is there in it for human activity?*

JS: That's my problem; that's my tightrope walk. I concern myself with the abstraction of the space, and making it beautiful. It goes without saying, of course, that making comfortable chairs and good reading lights is a part of the project. But I don't address myself to that immediately. I address myself first to the abstraction of the space.

BLDD: *Apparently you were a very good painter, then suddenly, along about 1965, you decided to give it up. What gave you the idea to be an interior designer and how did you go about it?*

JS: You have to understand, first of all, that it was painful being a painter. I was lonely. I wasn't married, and I was living in New York, which is a technological society. Everyone would go off to work in the morning but me. I wanted to get out and participate with other people. How I went about it was simply the way the *New York Times* always says. I read the want ads. I looked around until I found a position that I thought would be good for me, and I took it.

BLDD: *What was that?*

JS: It was with a small firm that's no longer in existence. I'm sure I contributed to that!

BLDD: *What did you do for them?*

JS: Everything. I did presentation boards; I ran around the corner to pick up samples; I designed the interiors. It was a small office, and in that respect it was good for me. I was able to learn everything from the ground up.

BLDD: *You were an apprentice in the age-old way.*

JS: Absolutely.

BLDD: *I can understand your wish to avoid the loneliness of painting—but is the gregariousness of interior designing ever a little more than you counted on?*

JS: Oh, yes. I probably went from one kind of pain to another.

BLDD: *Which pain is more pleasurable?*

JS: I'm not certain. You'd better ask me that in about ten years!

BLDD: *You started designing and painting almost at the same time—when you were a six-year-old, drawing on the back of your doctor father's prescription pads in Kansas City. Did your parents encourage you in your pursuits?*

JS: They humored me. I think six-year-olds are not taken that seriously. But, when I turned seven, they got serious. I remember a conversation I had with my father. He said, "You can be a doctor and have art as a hobby." And I said, no, I would be an artist and have medicine as a hobby.

BLDD: *How did the Saladino family ever get to Kansas City anyway?*

JS: In 1923, after my father had graduated from medical school in Italy, he moved to Kansas City. He said that professionals in Italy are a dime a dozen. My grandparents had taken a trip through the United States in the early part of this century, and had remarked upon what a beautiful city Kansas City was. The fountains must have reminded them of Europe.

BLDD: *Was there anything in your training as a painter that has particularly influenced your design work? I'm thinking especially of what most markedly characterizes your work—its sense of composition and its nuanced color.*

JS: I'm flattered that you would think that. I feel strongly that what I learned as a painter contributed to the way I approach the designing of a space. The color, absolutely, is important. I don't think you ever can put too much effort into orchestrating the color. If you're doing an environment, you have to con-

144

John F. Saladino

cern yourself not only with the color you choose, but with the implications of the color as it changes, through daylight, or at nighttime, with incandescent light. The interaction of colors is also important. I often tell clients that if they put a red rug in a white room, they'll end up with pink walls. The light that bounces off the red floor changes the wall color.

BLDD: *If one is familiar with the palette you use, it's hard to imagine that you would ever put a red rug in a white room. Colors like taupe and beige seem to be two of your favorites; they are an integral part of the calm effect that you want to create. Could you use a brighter and bolder palette and create the same results?*

JS: Oh, absolutely. I think that what you have to do, though, is use color that's appropriate to a given situation. There are clients who want more color. These clients are living or have offices in sunny parts of the world, and they enjoy more color. In a northern situation, such as New York, you can use less color. Serenity has a lot to do with color, but it also comes from not overdesigning—with holding back, with leaving empty spaces.

BLDD: *You have been known to say that it's not what you put into a room that's most important, but rather what you leave out! How do you strike that balance between the positive and the negative?*

JS: I tell the clients that it's very important to concern ourselves with the negative spaces and not just what we put in, because a room is not just a receptacle that you stuff with furnishings or with people. It's like a marriage. There has to be a balance, an equilibrium between what goes into the space and the container itself.

BLDD: *Most of us have a tendency to fill space with too much even when the better part of our taste and judgment says use a little bit less. You must have guidelines—what are your ground rules?*

JS: I banish lamps—those ugly ceramic things with big shades. They make the room look smaller than it really is, and they intrude upon the serenity of the space. I also sometimes reduce the scale of the furnishings. If you're dealing with a room with an eight-foot ceiling—which I refer to as a "walk-in filing cabinet for the living"—you have to do a lot to give people the sense that the room is actually elegant and tall.

BLDD: *As I see it, you'll have to give them something else, too. If you banish lamps, what do you do for light?*

JS: You certainly have to have good reading light, but you don't need a lamp with a drum shade. You must have three kinds of lighting in a room: ambient light, which is indirect light that illuminates the architecture; the light that you read or work by; and art light. By that I mean any light that is specific, such as the lighting of a stair, or a painting, or candles on a table.

BLDD: *Let's come back for a moment to the question of color. There are studies in color psychology that reveal a great deal: pale blue is said to be restful, red energizes, and I've heard that a certain shade of green is most often used to create a sense of "integrated wholeness." Can you tell us what color means to you?*

JS: Of course, no two people see one color the same way, but in my mind, a soft gray-green is extremely restful. There are greens and there are greens. Josef Albers once taught a course at Yale in which he pointed out that Coca-Cola produces bottle tops in two shades of red. There's a cool red in the south and a warm red in the north. Once he asked that all the students bring to class a two-by-two-inch square of the most intense red they could find. When thirty young people put their two-by-two-inch squares together, some appeared pink, some appeared brown. So it's also in the juxtaposition and in the quantity of the color.

BLDD: *Did you study with Albers?*

JS: I had his last class. I was lucky.

BLDD: *Were there any particular experiences that you had with him that have influenced your life or your career?*

JS: I think he taught me a lot about discipline—about the fact

145

that you sometimes have to use the finest of strainers. By that I mean that you have to be very particular. A lot of what designers do is editorial. We sift out hundreds of samples that come into the office every week. We examine all things that other people don't even think about: where the light switch is, what it looks like, how high off the floor it's located, and whether or not it should be the color of the wall. That is why I say that "God is in the details!"

BLDD: *Considering your training and your interests, would it be safe to assume that you regularly involve artists in collaborating with you in designing some interiors?*

JS: No, because we think of the interior itself as art. If I may be so egotistical, I am the artist. It would be a little foolish of me to go out and seek my competition. I regard the interior literally as art. I don't care about a chair in terms of its chairness. I'm concerned with it as an abstract shape. Remember— the interior is "a walk-in still life."

BLDD: *How did you ever get the idea to design a chair that is very comfortable to sit in?*

JS: I was frustrated, because I wanted an absolutely anonymous chair, with an absolutely abstract silhouette. And I wanted to get rid of the legs. One of the things I hate in dining rooms is a lot of legs. If you put eight chairs around a dining table and you multiply that by four, you've got thirty-two legs.

BLDD: *How do you solve that problem, unless everyone sits on the floor and eats from a tray?*

JS: I use my chair without legs as a dining chair.

BLDD: *How are the dining chairs upholstered?*

JS: I've done plush, I've also done leather. If you do leather with an analine finish, it's incredibly practical, because you can spill wine on analine-finished leather and wipe it right off. It's almost childproof!

BLDD: *You said earlier that your interiors are intended to be works of art. Can I then conclude that there is little room in your interiors for paintings or sculpture?*

JS: Oh, no. There are times when I don't feel that the wall has to be thought of as passive, but that we must hang a painting on it. For me, the wall sometimes functions in the room like "fluctuating figure ground," a concept you find in painting. We've had clients who are great collectors, and the entire environment has been built around their collections. I don't cringe or run from art, it's just that there are times when you do the positive, and times when you do the negative.

BLDD: *What if the client is also a collector of fine antique furniture? Must they junk their past in order to have John Saladino as a designer?*

JS: I think I've been typecast. Good antiques are wonderful. I like quality; I don't care whether it's new or old.

BLDD: *Your own collection includes some beautiful Korean bowls. Would you tell us how that collection of bowls would fit in with what has often been described as the "sensuous modernism" of your designs?*

JS: I regard the bowls, frankly, as sensual. They're corroded. The shapes are classic. They were probably in existence about the time Christ walked the earth. I like them not only because of their simple shapes, but also because of the corrosion and the color of the patina that's developed from being buried hundreds of years in a tomb. Because they are corroded, they are even more sensual. And I like the juxtaposition of them against a modern surface.

BLDD: *Who is the ideal client for you?*

JS: I used to say that a client who was involved was the ideal client. Now, I like the clients who leave me alone!

BLDD: *Are there any?*

JS: Yes, we have a wonderful client right now who lives in Rio de Janeiro!

BLDD: *What's a day in the office of John Saladino and his associates like?*

JS: It's like Hialeah. The gun goes off and the telephones start ringing, and all lines light up. And it's a little bit like plugging the holes in the dam: I run from one hole to the other and plug each the best way I can.

BLDD: *That sounds like a temporary solution, though.*

JS: We have tried to bring in efficiency experts, but they've had nervous breakdowns! Anyway, the end results are good and no one remembers the journey.

BLDD: *You've said that the most important requirement for a design is that it be appropriate for the client. How do you get inside clients' heads and try to determine what their needs are, when often they may not know themselves?*

JS: They do know what they are comfortable with. That will often bring them to the point of discussing a lot of things through the back door, so to speak. We ask for two lists, one headed "must," and one headed "maybe." That will tell us if they are allergic to wool, or want dining space for eight people, or how many people they want to seat comfortably in the living room. People who are past fifty want to sit differently from people under twenty-five.

BLDD: *What's the difference?*

JS: First of all, they want to sit more upright, and they don't want to need help getting in and out of the sofa. Young people often don't even like furniture. They often prefer, in fact, to lounge around on the floor. So you have to do what's appropriate to the age of the client.

BLDD: *I've often heard that good designers have to be psychoanalysts as well, and I noticed that your list includes "musts" and "maybes," but no "nevers." Don't you give them an option?*

JS: Oh, sure. Why not? I have a very well known client in California right now who has forbidden the office to use beige, which is a color I do like.

BLDD: *That may change the direction of your entire career.*

JS: I learn a lot from all the clients.

BLDD: *What are you learning from that particular client?*

JS: I've learned that there are more shades of white than I ever dreamed of!

BLDD: *Why do clients come to you?*

JS: I think because they are familiar with the work. They want an environment that's beautifully designed, and well engineered. It's a little bit like going to a good restaurant: they know that they will dine well.

BLDD: *Is it a confirmation of their taste?*

JS: In many cases, it is. And in some cases, I think that we're status symbols.

BLDD: *How does it feel to be a status symbol?*

JS: It's not uncomfortable. It's a little bit like fame—as long as you don't let it go to your head, you can cope with it.

BLDD: *How many clients does your office take on at any one time? Are you involved in at least the major aspects of every job that you do?*

JS: Absolutely. Right now we have about twenty-four clients. I personally design every environment—whether it's corporate or residential.

BLDD: *Why don't we talk about one of your trademarks, the quilted bedroll. How did you develop that idea?*

JS: When I was struggling and living in a loft, I purchased a double bed quilt from a department store, and I was trying to make it work on a single bed. So I simply rolled it up at the ends, sort of like a cowboy's sleeping blanket. That is where the idea started. Then I decided, "Well, why not?" So necessity *is* sometimes the mother of invention.

BLDD: *Considering the limitations on your time and the number of jobs that any one designer can do, you obviously have to restrict the number of clients you take. On what basis do you decide which jobs to accept or reject? And what's the minimum amount that a job can cost?*

JS: The minimum cost of a job that the office now takes is $100,000. It's not always easy to decide on the kind of clients and how you take them. Sometimes we'd like to take everybody, but we can't. You have to use your instincts. If, for instance, a client says, "I know what I like, but I don't have the time to do it," it isn't very nice, because in a way he's saying to you, "Look dummy, you just get what I tell you to get."

John F. Saladino
Living room
1980

That is the first thing that kind of puts me off.

BLDD: *What would a client with a two-bedroom apartment get for $100,000? How would that money be spent?*

JS: Of the $100,000, maybe $65,000 would go toward construction. The remaining money would go toward furnishings.

BLDD: *Obviously, the priority for you is redefining the space.*

JS: Absolutely. Most modern buildings, which I refer to as white glazed scourges on the landscape, are really not fit for human habitation. They are designed by default, by realtors, and they don't make even the slightest gesture toward making people comfortable. So what we have to do is to restructure. That includes all the lighting. In most apartment buildings, the windows are ugly, or positioned so high that you can only see the view if you're standing right at the window. We often find ourselves having to put in all new windows, or build some sort of platform that allows people to enjoy the view while they are seated. The doors are also often ugly. We always try to put in full-height doors, because they make a space much larger in feeling, and they're more elegant.

BLDD: *Suppose a young couple who had more taste than funds came to you and said, "We know your work, we admire it, and we would like to live in an environment that you've created." Could you do something for them?*

JS: I would recommend to them some people that once were part of our office, and send them there. The truth is that the overhead of running the office is such that we honestly cannot afford to take jobs for less than the budget we just discussed.

BLDD: *You've described the living room in one of your recent jobs, a beautiful East Side New York apartment, as "a white cathedral." What did you intend to create there—and do you think you've succeeded?*

JS: The white cathedral is one half of my concern, which is basically that there be the opportunity in each environment to satisfy every emotion. So I talk about the womb as well as the white cathedral. The womb is the space that you go to on cold afternoons when you want to curl up and feel protected from the elements. The white cathedral is where you go on a beautiful May morning when you wish you really weren't indoors; it's where you go to be as close as you can to not being sheltered. I always feel that it is very important to accomplish both these things in an environment. A small, dark entrance hall will make a white living room appear much larger.

BLDD: *Is that what you've done in that East Side apartment?*

JS: Not in that case, but that's what we often do. We squeeze people in through a tunnellike entrance. Arabs say that narrow is the passage to heaven. The entrance hall is a throwaway space—you don't live in it, so you make it very dramatic. And that juxtaposition will make an ordinary eight-foot living room ceiling appear much, much higher.

BLDD: *Can you describe how you juxtaposed the antique and the modern in that apartment that we just referred to?*

JS: That apartment was a little different from a lot of our work. Architecturally, it was already beautiful. Some things had been done to alter it, but nothing that we couldn't put back, so there we were passive. We were "restorators." Our role there was not to tear down, but to hold the client back. She had more beautiful antiques than most museums. So I had to act as kind of a "Dutch uncle." We used a minimalist attitude in an apartment which would have been opulent. We took the thunder out of the palace.

BLDD: *And with what did you replace it?*

JS: With a lot of twentieth-century furnishings that people would consider vernacular. The bookcases in the library were spray-lacquered with irridescent jukebox paint, which is a beautiful peacock feather color. We took all the velvet off her Queen Anne chairs and covered them with raincoat fabric. We began to make it a much more viable twentieth-century interior, even though all the antiques were of the finest quality.

BLDD: *Is it a job that particularly pleases you?*

JS: The client was wonderful, so she made the job wonderful. She was cultivated and willing to try new ideas.

BLDD: *What's the most difficult part of your work these*

148

John F. Saladino
"Pavilion" sofa
1981

days—cajoling the suppliers, arguing with the upholsterers, persuading the client?

JS: One problem always occurs; it usually has to do with the collapse of clients' trust in us. This usually happens after about three months. It's a little bit like being caught in traffic. They think that if they jump into a cab, the cab will somehow lift and fly over the traffic. But it doesn't happen. When the job is in progress, they get discouraged because they think it's going to go much more quickly than it does. We constantly warn them that everything in the apartment will be dirty except the inside of the refrigerator. But they don't remember that until they come home after a long day of hard work and walk into an apartment that's covered with dirt and dust. That's when their trust begins to collapse.

BLDD: *At what point does it pick up again?*

JS: About a month before they move in. So you have about four months of hand-holding.

BLDD: *What is the average duration of a job?*

JS: Eight months.

BLDD: *With all the difficulties—in dealing with the realities of urban life and in supplying the kind of services that you or your clients would like to have—it's understandable that more and more interior designers are devising strategies to mass market their products. Do you see this as a trend, and does it interest you?*

JS: In terms of making good design available to the public, yes. I'm obviously doing that. My chairs are now sold through Dunbar.

BLDD: *What is the cost of them through Dunbar versus their cost custom-made?*

JS: I think that they're about the same. I've forgotten, but I think the chairs are around $800. My feeling is that good design should be available to the American public. If you go into a department store in Italy, you can find the best design. In the United States, we can't do that.

BLDD: *Wasn't there a John Saladino collection for Blooming-*

dale's, about which you said that you were offering "Maseratis at Buick prices"? What's the fundamental difference between a Maserati and a Buick, in terms of construction, fabric, scale and price?

JS: The difference is in the engineering and in the finishing. The furniture at Bloomingdale's did not have five coats of hand-rubbed, high-gloss lacquer. Nor was it Carpathian elm burl. It was laminated in Formica. That's how we were able to preserve the design, and take some of the cost out of the furniture.

BLDD: *Are you still designing things for a mass market?*

JS: Yes. But they will not be available through the department stores, I regret to say, unless things change, except for my outdoor furniture, which will be sold through Lord & Taylor.

BLDD: *Why would that be the case?*

JS: They're two worlds, and I can't get them together. I've tried.

BLDD: *If stores are in business to sell more and more of whatever it is that they're selling, why can't the two get together?*

JS: I think it's simply because rigor mortis set in a long time ago, and the department stores have access to factories in North Carolina which do not hire outside name designers. There's always the problem that they will lose control by having an outside designer, so it doesn't happen very often.

BLDD: *But why aren't large companies more interested in trying to offer good design by a well-known designer?*

JS: The first thing they'll tell you about is the difference between design and merchandising.

BLDD: *What is that difference?*

JS: "Merchandising" is a mask for mediocrity. I begged the people at Corning to take those awful blue flowers off their pots. The problem really is that you cannot get people on the marketing end of the business—whether they are the purchasing agents or whatever—to come around to your thinking. They have made up their minds that vinyl lounges in the colo-

149

John F. Saladino
"Papyrus" chair
1981

John F. Saladino
"Corolla" chair
1982

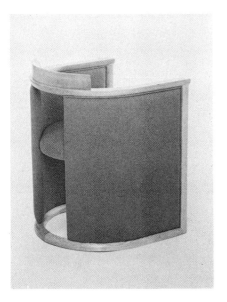

nial style will outsell my chairs.

BLDD: *Several years ago, when the Formica Corporation decided to try and make Formica available to a wider public, it commissioned eighteen well-known designers, offering a respectable stipend of about $5,000, and asked each one to come up with a new use for Formica. As someone who, before then, had usually thought in terms of mirror and steel and lacquer and so on, what did you invent for Formica?*

JS: I used the furniture that I designed for Bloomingdale's as a vehicle for putting forward my thoughts on what can be done with plastic laminates. There's nothing to be ashamed of with plastic. What I hate are plastics that are made to look like what they're not—walnut or marble. We tried to show the public that there's nothing the matter with laminate. And we also tried to convince them that Formica can be used in other rooms besides the kitchen. That was my contribution.

BLDD: *Have you ever used it in the living room?*

JS: Absolutely.

BLDD: *On a non-budget job?*

JS: On a non-budget job.

BLDD: *How do you do that?*

JS: Very simple. It looks just like that most expensive lacquer, except it's much more practical.

BLDD: *You've said that there is such a thing as vulgar scale. What does that mean?*

JS: Vulgar scale? Overdone, exaggerated. The kind of things that you see from time to time: nine-foot-long sofas that become grotesque, lamps that are six feet high, chairs that it would take four men to move.

BLDD: *Could you come up with an elegant use for almost any building material or fabric?*

JS: I don't see why not. I think proportions and juxtaposition, can carry a lot of materials that we think of as humble.

BLDD: *Do you use any of those so-called humble materials?*

JS: I use wire glass, which is thought of as industrial. And I like it. I've used it for floor-to-ceiling dividers in offices. I'm trying to use it for the tops of a series of low tables.

BLDD: *What are your newest ideas for branching out to areas of design that would free you, on the one hand, from dependence on your private clients, and, on the other hand, give you the time that you need to start painting again?*

JS: Obviously, we all want to invent a money machine. Wouldn't it be nice to turn it on every morning? I'm hoping that the sale of the furnishings I have designed for Dunbar and Meadowcraft and David Edwards will give me a cushion— a hedge against the burden of taking on so much private work.

BLDD: *Earlier, you mentioned your outdoor furniture. Are you designing a new line of furniture, and can you describe it?*

JS: I'm doing the furniture very much the way I do the upholstery. I'm trying to rid chairs of legs. I'm making the chair extremely comfortable, and one that you can leave outside all the time. It will be done in a kind of woven steel mesh. Some will be "powder coated," which means that it's covered in a white vinyl skin. We're also going to make the chair available in a matte finish stainless steel. Then I'm trying to work on my quilted bedroll, so that you can leave it outdoors. We would like to use parachute nylon. And instead of down or dacron, it would be filled with tiny foam pellets.

BLDD: *How do you live at home?*

JS: We have one son, Graham. We live pretty much the way people don't expect us to live.

BLDD: *Does that mean like all the rest of us?*

JS: I suppose so. We bought a beautiful apartment, and I keep saying that I am going to remodel it in the summer, when my wife and son go to the country. That was five years ago. Graham's room is quite ghastly.

BLDD: *Did he design it?*

JS: It's design by default. It happened. He moves the furniture around quite often. He has ugly little decals all over the walls and the bathroom door, trophies everywhere, pictures of school classmates. It's a very human environment.

BLDD: *How do you restrain yourself from intruding upon it?*
JS: I committed mental suicide about four years ago. Now I don't even see it when I walk in his room.
BLDD: *How does he feel about the rest of the house?*
JS: He's not intimidated by any part of our environment. He uses it at will. We have stacked mattresses in the living room, and he will run across them if I'm not in the room.
BLDD: *Is that what you had in mind for that environment?*
JS: No, I did *not* have that in mind.
BLDD: *Now that you see it used that way, how do you transfer that information to the lives, and the environments, of your clients?*
JS: I have found that analine-finished leather and slipcovers are the panacea for families with young children.
BLDD: *So your apartment is a living laboratory?*
JS: It really isn't a laboratory—it's just a mess.
BLDD: *I know that you are sacrificing accuracy for humor, but can one say that a Saladino environment produces a favorable psychological effect? It sounds to me rather desirable that your son not be intimidated by your occupation.*
JS: I've discussed that with my wife. I said, "I wonder if he would be so normal if we had done this apartment as I had wanted to?" I frankly think, though, he has such a strong personality that no matter what we do to the apartment, he would still be the same person. I think that much of what he is, is what my wife and I have brought to him.
BLDD: *If that's the case, can one then conclude that perhaps the design of an environment doesn't affect us as much as we sometimes think it does?*
JS: Oh, it does. It does. It's a little bit like clothing. If you're well dressed, wearing a tuxedo or an evening gown, you act more properly than if you're in jeans. In an environment, I think, you act somewhat the same. A room that's beautifully furnished and appointed tends to quiet down the people's movements. It doesn't intimidate children, because children don't know what things cost, and they don't understand all the

work that goes into it. We have an extremely rare oriental carpet, and my son runs across it as though it were sisal.
BLDD: *Does the use of antiques in your home and in your recent designs for other apartments signify a new direction in your work? How has the current movement toward historical revivalism involved you?*
JS: I've been putting historical references in my work since the day I started. I think living in Rome for a year, as well as having parents of European origin, brought a lot to bear on my present sensibility. Something from the past makes us connect with the past. We're not born in a vacuum. And a room that's totally furnished with twentieth-century pieces lacks some of the richness that I think life should be about.
BLDD: *Much of your design does, though, rely on a modernist tradition. In the light of what you say now, do you think people like Walter Gropius and Mies Van der Rohe would think of you as an inheritor or a violator of this tradition?*
JS: I walk a tightrope, because the shell and the architecture of my interiors are very modern. But how I furnish the interior often depends upon the client, too. If I choose to bring in period chairs and an antique carpet, I'm sure Gropius would say I was a violator. Mies would not. Those two are both considered great modernists, but, in his own apartment, Mies had an eighteenth-century Irish hunt table.
BLDD: *You said recently that you see yourself as the creator of gardens that have to be looked after and weeded every day. That calls to mind Voltaire's "cultivating one's own garden." Did you mean to say that our houses are our gardens, our own private places?*
JS: I think so. And you have to weed them. That has to do with change. There always has to be newness brought in—fresh flowers, a change of magazines and papers on the table.
BLDD: *It also implies a certain kind of precision and responsibility on the part of the occupant. Do you expect that?*
JS: I hope for it. I don't always see it.
BLDD: *How do you feel when clients start rearranging the*

151

John F. Saladino
"Sectioned Column" table
1981

furniture once you're out of there?

JS: That shouldn't happen very often. If you involve clients in the beginning, and plan the space so that the furnishings really work for them, there should be no reason for rearranging the whole room. That's not to say they can't change the objects or the paintings, or take a tree out, or whatever. I think a space should have some inherent, lasting qualities.

BLDD: *The Homestead Inn, which overlooks Long Island Sound in Greenwich, Connecticut, is in many ways different from other projects of yours, because it relies so heavily on historicism. This eighteenth-century inn was close to collapse when you first encountered it. What made you decide to take on that assignment?*

JS: First of all, let me say that my wife and I did that project together. We did not approach it like anything else we had ever done. I saw it strictly as a restoration. Our role was to put back what had been pulled, undo what had been done to brutalize the environment. In that respect, I didn't bring to it the same philosophy I'd bring to other work.

BLDD: *What did you do there?*

JS: We restored the building as closely as we could to what we thought it was like in 1840.

BLDD: *And how did you ensure historical accuracy?*

JS: In the process of remodeling, I finally abandoned half of the drawings. As we pulled down acoustical tile ceilings, we would expose cornices from 1840, and often the cornices revealed the original dimensions of the room. And, in pulling up the wall-to-wall carpeting, and then later the nineteenth-century floorboards, the eighteenth-century floorboards underneath showed us where the original walls and staircase were.

BLDD: *Have you worked on any other preservation projects?*

JS: I have done two others.

BLDD: *I think that's certainly different from what most people associate with John Saladino's interests. Can you tell us something about them?*

152 JS: It has to do with the client. The Homestead Inn was brought to us by a wonderful client for whom we'd done very modern offices. I was not about to turn down a very good client. That's how I got into it. We were also asked recently to restore the oldest house in Lakeville, Connecticut, built in 1722. That has been a slow-moving, tweezering kind of project. I've enjoyed it.

BLDD: *Do you think it will have a long-term effect on the rest of your work?*

JS: The same person who falls in love with the corrosion on old pots also has a tremendous love for old wood. There's a duality: one half of me likes the precision and skill that goes into the highly technical twentieth-century environment; the other half likes to break all the rules and to use wood that was obviously hand-planed.

BLDD: *How do you describe yourself—as an interior designer, interior decorator, a space planner, an artist, or all of the above?*

JS: Well, right now we're doing architecture. So I don't put a label on, I just say we do everything. There are three architects in the office, and we are doing architecture.

BLDD: *When you say you're doing architecture, is it only the redefining of space to which you're referring, or designing the actual structure itself?*

JS: We're now designing our third house from the ground up. It's in Old Westbury, and it will be thought of as a modern ruin—although it's becoming less and less of a ruin and more and more modern. The client doesn't like the idea of broken columns in the garden. I think they will definitely go.

BLDD: *What was your intent with the broken columns?*

JS: The idea was that the house should not be presented in the landscape as a finished structure, but, rather, almost existentially, as a chunk of a time continuum. I wanted to suggest that the house was a fragment of what was once much bigger or in fact could be bigger. The idea was that the house be presented not as a finished object, but as something in transition. . . .

John F. Saladino
Dining room
1980

155

John F. Saladino
Dining room
1980

John F. Saladino
Study
1980

John F. Saladino
Living room
1980

John F. Saladino
Guest room/study
1980

John F. Saladino
Bedroom
1980

John F. Saladino
Dining room
1980

Following page:
John F. Saladino's living room
1981

BLDD: *Robert A. M. Stern is a designer, teacher, exhibition organizer, writer and lecturer—an impresario of the first rank. What's the best kind of client to have for all that wonderful work that you do?*

RAMS: First, I suppose, a client must have enough money to spend on the project. But since nobody ever has enough, we can go on past that point: I think that the best clients are those who have ideas about what they want and are able to articulate them. It helps if clients have enough distance from themselves and from their ideas to be able to recognize that when they hire someone, an architect or an interior designer or whomever, they are entering into a professional relationship. The best clients are the ones who don't confuse their architects with their psychiatrists.

BLDD: *What is the starting point of a design for you?*

RAMS: There is no one starting point. I think that what is needed is always paramount. It's not just the functional aspects of a job that are interesting; clearly, that's very boring. In *one* way or another, houses or office buildings are alike. There is another dimension to it, which is to try to understand what aspirations the owner, or the client, has for the project. If the client comes to an architect or a designer, he wants something more than just shelter; he wants to express something about himself. That is the hard part: to understand what the client wants, and to suggest that he has certain responsibilities that he may not even be aware of. That's the professional part; architecture is a cultural act, you don't just build things willy-nilly. You build them in an appropriate way, with the architect and the client working together. Only then is it possible to interpret the whole range of a situation and make something good.

BLDD: *How often does that happen? And what happens when your statement differs from that which the client wants, or thinks he wants, to make?*

RAMS: Usually I get fired. Barring that, the client sometimes realizes that perhaps I do have something to contribute that he or she hadn't thought about. The best clients realize that they come to an architect to get something that they hadn't themselves imagined. In the case of domestic architecture and interiors, people often come with armloads of the latest clippings from magazines—even clippings of my own work. And then they say, "Do it that way, do it this way." I try to say, "Why does that interest you?" The hard part is, of course, that none of us wants to imitate each other, and certainly none of us wants to repeat ourselves. On the other hand, we don't want to make things that are opportunistically innovative, just for the sake of calling attention to ourselves in the magazines. So you have to have ideas of your own as an architect or a designer before the client comes to your office. You can't invent architecture, or how to do it, with the client sitting there at the table.

BLDD: *You are an architect, not an interior designer, yet you do many interiors. How does your role differ from that of a designer or a decorator or a space planner, if a job involves only interior work?*

RAMS: I don't know what "space planning" is. I think that's something in NASA. I love interior decoration. Rooms have walls, windows and moldings. All that paraphernalia describes a room, lends a character to it. But the room needs other things that are not part of the architecture—furniture, decoration, something on the walls—to complete the ensemble. A decorator, in the old sense, can help to bring things together and assemble fabrics. The architect can act as a decorator. Stanford White was a great decorator. That doesn't mean that he was better or worse than his contemporary Elsie de Wolfe. But they both approached decoration on decorative terms. Interior design is another matter. I think interior design was invented when architects stopped making rooms that had character—when they said that a room was merely a box, a white walled cube. Or, preferably, not even a box, but a sort of interlocking series of volumes that one moves through. People were then forced to inhabit these rooms in some way or

160

Robert A.M. Stern

another, whether for work or their private lives. And the architect said, "Call up the Museum of Modern Art, get a Miró tapestry, get a Calder, get a Barcelona chair," and so forth. Clearly, it isn't enough, so interior designers came in to fix the place up. I don't need, in my own work, an interior designer in that sense. I love to work with people who decorate spaces that I seek to create, and once in a while I succeed at it.

BLDD: *You've been described as one of the leading exponents of post-modernism. Just what is meant by that term—and is the word still in use?*

RAMS: The term "post-modernism" is an invention of the devil, since no one wants to be categorized in a narrow way. But it does refer to the situation in architecture now, in which there is a reaction against the kind of abstract, empty white interiors, or gridded, noncommunicative, self-referential exterior architecture of the 1950s and '60s. There is a desire to return to the larger tradition of architecture—not to revive it, because no one can ever really revive anything. But we want to look again at the work of the past, classicism in particular, but also various vernacular styles, to see them afresh, to recombine them in new programs, new situations, new techniques. We want to forge a synthesis that bespeaks our time, but also makes connections to the past, so that it does not seem strident or iconoclastic.

BLDD: *What is the origin of the term? It's been around for almost forty years.*

RAMS: It's a term that exists in historiography, the writing of history. After World War II, Arnold Toynbee observed that we were in a post-modern epoch because of the bomb and the devastation of the war, and so forth. Things were different. The term is also used, with different interpretations, in literature and the plastic arts; now it is used in architecture and design. Post-modernism is not *against* what we used to call Modern architecture, the modernism of the '20s to the '50s. We are looking at the architecture of the recent past with critical eyes, sorting out things that have genuine value, as opposed to things we supported for ideological reasons. But post-modernism is not trying to throw tradition overboard, as modernism did.

BLDD: *Do you see everything as continuous?*

RAMS: Yes. In the broad sense, there is Renaissance and post-Renaissance architecture and it continues all the way through. These movements, post-modernism, modernism, are all different historical movements within a continuum.

BLDD: *So are you saying that the modern period began in the fifteenth century?*

RAMS: Correct.

BLDD: *And that there is a continuity from that point until this most recent period, called the modernist period. And, in the evolution of that thinking, we are now in the post-modernist period. According to your description of the present time, we are currently involved with more and more ornament. If this is the case, what differentiates your work now from other interior designers—for example, the work of Mario Buatta, or Albert Hadley, or Denning and Fourcade, all of whom are interested in ornament and decoration?*

RAMS: That's a broad range of designers. In some ways, I think, we have in common an interest in the ornamented room. The fundamental difference is, I think, that some of those people are not interior designers as I would define it, but decorators, and their emphasis is on the selection of objects, fabrics and other paraphernalia of interior decoration to complete an architectural ensemble. Often, the architecture itself is about as spirited and interesting as a white box apartment on Third Avenue. It doesn't connect in a deep way with any meaning beyond the tactile, pleasurable effects of surface. I am not against decoration; and no one, I think, who's interested in art can deny its importance. To make art in the genuine sense, as opposed to making decor, one has to connect up with broad traditions, principles of composition, and not wander among various stylistic subtastes—French Provincial today, Regency tomorrow.

161

BLDD: *Do you see antiques as paraphernalia? Do you ever use them?*

RAMS: Yes, often. And often we use semi-antiques from the early modernist period, like craftsman furniture or rattan furniture for summer porches, to heighten the architectural ideas of the project; to make manifest in a concrete way things that a building—which is basically inarticulate—cannot.

BLDD: *Why don't we talk about some of your specific jobs. One interior that has many of the aspects of a house is Jerome Greene Hall at the Columbia University School of Law. What were you trying to do there?*

RAMS: We were trying to make a room for the school and the university. The law school at Columbia is in an utterly characterless building of the 1950s. It has about as much sense of an academic institution and the pillars of the law as the Port Authority Bus Terminal. The law school acquired the use of the former Women's Faculty Club at Columbia, which was an okay building of the mid-'20s, and which has been used for a hundred other things since. The strategy was to reintroduce the kind of character that was appropriate both to the Women's Faculty Club and to the idea of a law school student facility. My impression, after some conversation with the faculty and the students, was that most law students were really just preparing for Wall Street—that is, for the moment when they would graduate and join the University Club or wherever. So we tried to make an environment that spoke of that, yet was done on a modest budget and in a simple, slightly ironic way. The furniture selected was big and four-square and covered in vinyl, but evoked the shapes of club chairs in a downtown club. An ornamental program was introduced to pick up on some of the details of the building and to suggest a kind of Adamesque quality in the interior.

BLDD: *Obviously, there are some Stern hallmarks in that space. Perhaps you might talk about some of the architectural detail that distinguishes the room as the work of your fine hand and reflects what it is that you had in mind.*

162

Robert A. M. Stern
Perspective drawings for bedroom
1979

RAMS: What you really should see is that someone understood the proportions and inherent character of the room, and interpreted them in relation to the kind of room that once was there. It was a kind of Adamesque room to begin with. But I saw Adam with a fresh eye, with a plywood eye, if you will. The room wasn't designed for the few decorous ladies who had the courage to teach in a men's university in 1925, but for the men and women who are law students now. The transition between past and present was made through the use of certain molding, certain panels, the relatively delicate but not fey color scheme, and so forth. And a reproduction oriental carpet on the floor, I have to confess.

BLDD: *I also notice the absence of benevolent benefactors. Where are all the usual ponderous portraits?*

RAMS: We didn't have any. They've kept every decent portrait locked away since 1968, so all we had were the ones no one would want. But there was a nice benefactor who bought good art from the galleries. It was modernist art, very abstract. And we encouraged them to buy a few things by Lichtenstein and so forth, which at least have figural representation. It is that ensemble across time that I, at least, favor.

BLDD: *Are there any lessons from that space that can be applied to the design of homes?*

RAMS: If you're talking about renovation, the building, no matter what building you're working with, has a character. It is better to try to roll with the punches than fight them. You try to learn what the building means, what the architect had in mind, and then take it from there. If you're building a new structure, the only thing I could say is that a white box with an aspirant triangle for a roof is not my idea of home. I think that the great traditions of architecture have a certain continuity. Columns have entasis because columns with tapered shapes are more beautiful than straight columns. And a column without a capital and a base isn't a column at all, but a pipe supporting a roof. My respect has increased for those architects who, freed of the telephone and memos and harry-

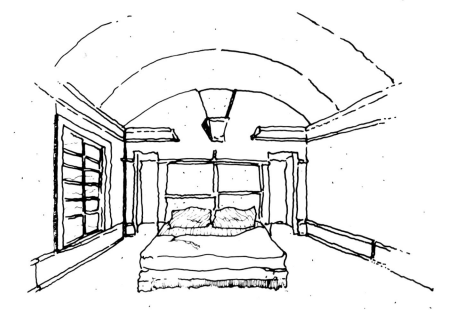

ing airplane rides and so forth, could sit in their offices or their studios a hundred or five hundred years ago, and spend all their time worrying about the shape of the column. This is certainly not the way I was educated in architecture.

BLDD: *Is that possible any longer?*

RAMS: It had better become possible again. I'm trying, but there are distractions. The next best thing is to learn what is already known and to start from that point—not to start by staring at your navel for inspiration, which was the way I was taught to study architecture.

BLDD: *Your own apartments have been widely published and are quite well known. I'm talking about an early apartment on Central Park West with curving platforms and a later one which, with curving and diagonal walls, is a dramatic change from the original floor plan of the 1920s building. You once said that Philip Johnson described this second one as the quintessential 1960s apartment. Can you tell us what he, and you, meant by that?*

RAMS: On the one hand, it was definitely a modernist work. It had white walls, stripped down to some extent. Many of the details of the original—a nondescript apartment, big, but boring, of the '20s—were retained. But the way the apartment was remodelled spatially was to make odd cuts through the plan—big curving walls, for example—to move people through the spaces in a way that the original architect had never intended them to move. Those cuts were made in the most dramatic way, so that you sensed that a real slice had been made through a thick wall. There was no attempt to be subtle. Furniture was placed on the diagonal, pictures were hung in strange relationships and, in the case of the first one, with the platform, closer to the floor than normal. The idea there was to make a dialogue between past and present, but the dialogue was more a confrontational than a conversational one.

BLDD: *Would you do either of those jobs the same way again?*

RAMS: Absolutely not.

BLDD: *What would you do otherwise now?*

RAMS: I still think that the original plan of the second Central Park West apartment was lousy. A lousy plan is just a lousy plan. But I would try to reshape that series of spaces as a kind of Georgian apartment, with walls and pertinent details that are more sympathetic to the inherent character of the building. I would make new moldings, and I would put new chair rails in the rooms if I thought they were appropriate. I would try to be spatially innovative, but not eccentric, which was part of the '60s thing.

BLDD: *How would you describe the quintessential 1980s apartment? Is it interpretive, imitative? What is it?*

RAMS: It's emulative—if I were to put a label on it. It seeks either to emulate or reconstitute the character the building might have had, or that the architect of the building might have wanted for the individual apartment had he been able to design it in any detail. Most architects who design apartment buildings don't really get to do very much on the inside, no matter how much money or attention they are able to lavish on the facade. It might also be a case where the building has no character. I'm currently doing an apartment in a building of the 1950s on East End Avenue that really has no character whatsoever. Maybe another generation will see a character that I'm unable to see; I see it as a brick box of mediocre construction. We're trying to create an environment for those rooms which is simple and rather spare, because the ceilings are low and the character of the windows (which we can't change) is as it is. We are using moldings and chair rails and details in the cabinetwork. When you do interiors, the details are incredibly important and very hard to talk about. I want them to suggest another realm of ideas, of grandeur and more solid architecture.

BLDD: *From what I understand, a great deal of work is repeat work, so to speak: the happy and satisfied client who returns for more.*

RAMS: One dreams of this always. Yes.

163

BLDD: *Let us say there is a client of the 1970s whose life and space and work ten years later have changed. In addition, it is time to have the environment freshened up, repainted, whatever. But he or she is not prepared, either intellectually or financially, to make the leap forward that you have made. What do you do when you're called back?*

RAMS: I can tell an amusing story along those lines. I did an apartment seven or eight years ago in a very unusual building facing Fifth Avenue. It was a very good example of a kind of clean, clear modernism. It was a duplex apartment with a very elaborate staircase that was almost a room on two floors. Some other people wished to buy that apartment, but were unable to. Instead, they found an almost identical one in the only other building in New York where that would be possible. And they hired me to repeat the first presumed success.

BLDD: *Were you willing to do so?*

RAMS: No, I didn't want to do that. They're very good, intelligent clients, because they didn't fire me. They said, "What *do* you want to do?" And they put me through the correct hoops, asking me questions like those you're asking me, about why I didn't want to do what I had done before. I was able to say that not only was I seven years older and seven years wiser, but that my beliefs had changed and grown as a result of my experience. I think that anybody who doesn't change that way and make things and do them better, or differently—experiment, in short—is operating in a rut. I think you should expect people to change. Whether it's random shifting about from one style or color to another, or whether it is true growth, is a matter, I suppose, for the individual to determine.

BLDD: *Should a space, or an apartment, reflect the lifestyle of the occupants, and their presumed needs? Or should it really be designed in terms of certain abstract or real emotions of the architect, who must then bring the client along? That does smack of the missionary . . .*

RAMS: Yes, but that's missionary in terms of the modernism of the '20s. We were told then that modern architecture was

164

Robert A. M. Stern
Perspective drawing for bathroom
1979

better for us, that we would be better people for living with no objects in white rooms with no curtains on the windows; that all that sunshine would make us healthy. All it did was give us high energy bills and headaches. I'm not a missionary in that sense. But I think it's clear that I couldn't be a professional (and I take that term very seriously) if I did not bring to the work certain ideas and principles about the composition of walls, rooms, windows, what have you, that are not just about immediate concerns, lifestyle or whatever. I think you can have a good time in a palace, and you can have a good time in the subways of New York. I don't believe architecture improves people's lives.

BLDD: *There is a work that you've done recently: that you must think can improve our lives, or at least make them more pleasant. It is a bedroom in East Hampton that you refer to as the "Temple of Love."*

RAMS: I didn't think it would improve anything. It was just done to honor an occasion, that's all. I'm not into sex therapy or psychiatry!

BLDD: *The Temple of Love has become, for you, a clue to your exploration of classical themes. Will you describe for us what your intent was in the Temple of Love, and how that has progressed since the original design?*

RAMS: The Temple of Love is nothing more nor less than a gentle renovation of an ordinary bedroom in an ordinary single-story house in East Hampton, which has slight classical aspirations about ninety-seven removes from the source. There was a wonderful view out to a garden, and we needed to make something as simple as the bed and a headboard. This rather dreary room had no character. We put some molding in, we tied together certain doors and gave them axial relationships that they didn't really have, and we blocked out others that seemed in the way. The long and short of it was to make the headboard as though it were made of keystones, but to upholster the keystones and then to use some columns, and carry a cornice across to give a kind of presence to the struc-

ture. Most furniture that's interesting, it seems to me—and in that sense the bed and headboard are pieces of furniture—are miniaturizations of architecture. Philip Johnson's AT&T Building is not a blown-up Chippendale highboy. A Chippendale highboy is a reduced version of a building with a split pediment on it. I don't know why people don't understand that; it's a simple fact of history. Johnson is merely returning to that architectural mode. The headboard was an opportunity to explore certain classical themes at a very small scale that I could comprehend, do rather quickly, and test the waters once again. Since then, I've done projects on many different scales; one was a Greek temple facade for Best Products that comments on the meaning of shopping in our society.

BLDD: *Shopping is a sacred ritual for lots of people...*

RAMS: It's a sacred ritual but, of course, the Best Products company denies us that ritual since you sit at home, pick out your television or whatever from a catalogue, then go there and hand them a little card with a number, give them money or another little plastic card, and out comes a television. You put it in your car, drive it home and consume it. All the pleasure of Madison Avenue is denied you. But it's cheap. I've used the temple theme to comment on this process.

BLDD: *Your work often is an architecture about architecture. You use a lot of historical and classic elements, such as you did in your recent proposal for the Chicago Tribune tower. Won't you tell us something about the Chicago Tribune competition?*

RAMS: There was a competition in 1922 in Chicago for the design of the world's most beautiful tall building, which was won by a firm called Howells and Hood, from New York. The structure was built much as they designed it, in the Gothic style. All the entries to the competition were published in a very thick book. It was a much ballyhooed competition at the time, and has become an important landmark in the evolution away from traditional architecture toward modernism. The recent competition was a fake; it was just an invitational

thing for architects to compose what they would do today for an exhibition.

BLDD: *Many of your buildings and interiors represent a composite of fragments, and what emerges in your competition design is an unexpected combination of the past and present and future. Can you tell us what you had in mind for your Chicago Tribune tower? Which architects in the earlier competition does your design most respond to?*

RAMS: Architecture is always about architecture, as is any discipline that has its own integrity. My design is about the Adolf Loos entry to the competition, which was also a giant column, and which, in turn, was based on Louis Sullivan's observation that the tall building is really a classical column. In fact, the tall building can also be an analogue for an erect human being.

BLDD: *But the sky column is historically one of the oldest metaphors for tall buildings.*

RAMS: Absolutely. We are emerging from a period in which the crackerjack box was the analogy. But up until recently, architectural elements were the basic references.

BLDD: *Tell us about the past, present and future in your design.*

RAMS: The past is the column, fairly faithfully shown in its adapted Tuscan order. The columns keep piling up. They're handled as pilasters, as in Michelangelo's use of the orders. And the raking cornice on the top is Michelangelesque. It is of the present in that it is a true office building. If you look around the back, you can see that it's just a square tower. It's sheathed in reflective glass of the kind that's all over our cities. The glass is used not merely to reflect nice buildings around it, but to help establish a real character for the building itself. By changing colors at the corners and in other parts of the design, one begins to emulate stone architecture in glass, and suggest some of the techniques that architecture traditionally has used to organize itself in space.

BLDD: *Is the use of a column for a newspaper building a bit*

of a pun, also?
RAMS: Oh, yes. Newspapers are printed in columns. People who work for newspapers are called columnists. But the pun should be attributed to Loos, not to me, because it is deliberate in his scheme. Loos is the man who compared ornament to crime. (In truth he never said it quite that way.)
BLDD: *Are you advocating a return to an earlier past here, as well?*
RAMS: I think that the buildings and rooms we admire are usually those of the past. We're now beginning to rather like modernism; people get all weepy-eyed for Eileen Gray at the Museum of Modern Art. They think they're having a contemporary experience. We appreciate things from the past because time brings meanings to artifacts. They accrue meaning—the madeleines of Proust. I would say that I am by no means the only architect who is trying to make lithic that sensibility for the past while, at the same time, building buildings and dealing with the ordinary problems that we all have as we try to get things done.

If I could editorialize slightly, I find it amusing that all the interior design magazines are filled with stuff that architects stopped doing twenty years ago. There are more modernist interiors being done by interior designers than architects ever did.
BLDD: *How do we do something about that lag between the architect and the designer? Can we, or should we?*
RAMS: Everybody should listen to *me!* And hire me, of course.
BLDD: *What would you advocate?*
RAMS: I would advocate taking all the stuff out of the attic that you threw up there, getting yourselves off the floor and back into chairs.
BLDD: *That's not what you told us twenty years ago.*
RAMS: I never told you to sit on cushions on the floor. I did that only once, and my back broke and I never did it again.
BLDD: *Okay. Here we are, emptying the attic.*
166 RAMS: Emptying the attics of your houses and of your minds; the attics of your houses I don't care about, but I am concerned about your mind.
BLDD: *Are all oldies goodies?*
RAMS: Survival is a very important factor in art. Witness the interest now in nineteenth-century art. I'm talking about the vast landscape paintings, or the sculpture of Remington, which any good child of the Museum of Modern Art, as I am, thought—was told—wasn't art.
BLDD: *Is that also a function of scarcity, and a burgeoning middle class that is collecting, with less and less material available at an affordable price?*
RAMS: No, absolutely not. It's part of the revisionist history of every field. We continue to make things, and there is plenty to collect, so that's not really the issue. As we begin to look back at modernist work, we realize we were told a lot of stuff that clearly can't be true.
BLDD: *But couldn't more be too much?*
RAMS: I don't think, in the way of ideas, more can ever be too much. It's true that your brain can get saturated at the end of the day, and you need a rest. But it doesn't require putting yourself into an empty white room with one calla lily and one cushion. I don't think that's rest. That's Zen mysticism.
BLDD: *What you are advocating, I assume, is more ideas of quality. But I suspect that the anti-clutter vogue was not just a reaction against the accumulation of objects and paraphernalia, but against a kind of messy-mindedness as well.*
RAMS: I think that's too easy. I think it was a kind of Calvinist, moralist puritanism that came out, as best as I can interpret it, at the end of the First World War. It was a European movement, reflecting a tremendous disillusionment with all that the Victorian and Edwardian sensibilities had brought about. People wanted to clean their houses in the hope of having a better world. The tall building, the crystalline tower, was actually seen, in conjunction with bureaucracy, as liberating. It's hard to believe, because we now see bureaucracy as anything but liberating, and we see the tower isolated from

Robert A. M. Stern
Apartment, plan and interior
elevations
1979

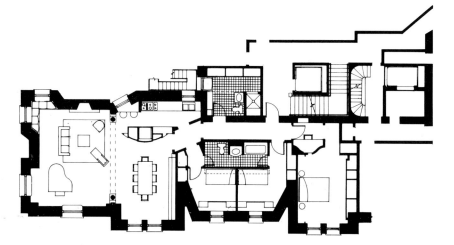

the city as alienating. It was seen differently in the 1920s in Germany and France. Form stays alive and meanings change. The forms of classicism have always been there, but their meanings change as they are inherited. That is the interesting part. The reason I like the forms of the past, whether classical or vernacular, is because they didn't evolve in a day. They are inextricably bound to a long process of search. I would like to participate in and continue that search. I don't really want to invent a new shape tomorrow morning. It would not be a good one, if I did.

BLDD: *But you would like to apply traditional shape to a new use.*

RAMS: That's right.

BLDD: *The design of furniture for some of the projects that you are currently involved in also relies on the use of classical columns. Can you tell us something about that?*

RAMS: I would say that in the history of architecture many shapes have been used interestingly for furniture. Architectural elements in compressed or reduced form are very beautiful. I have been experimenting with the use and interpretation of the column; I think the column furniture will go into production in a year or so.

BLDD: *Who will produce that for you?*

RAMS: Knoll is working on it; one problem is to find a new way to make the furniture. Knoll has pioneered in all kinds of techniques to mass-produce art furniture.

BLDD: *Do they have any furniture that resembles what you're talking about?*

RAMS: They have brought into the fold new people to do furniture. Stanley Tigerman is doing furniture for them, as well. I know that our projects have some similar themes, but we're not allowed to see each other's designs. Robert Venturi and Richard Meier are also doing furniture.

BLDD: *Much of your work involves architecture, of course, not just interiors. You're especially well known for houses that derive from the Shingle Style. Can you tell us what that means? And how literal are you in your reuse of history?*

RAMS: The Shingle Style is that architecture we associate with Eastern summer resorts—in particular, the work of H. H. Richardson, and the early work of McKim, Mead & White, before they started to do grand Newport palaces, houses in the older parts of resort communities there and elsewhere. It is an interesting style because it is an illustration of an attitude held a hundred years ago, and similar to one I believe in now. It combined clear room-planning that was basically classical with a composition that relied on the irregular massing of early saltbox cottages. Shingled roofs come down low to the ground, windows are eccentrically placed, chimneys are pronounced, and so forth. The Shingle Style was made possible by the new technology of the mid-nineteenth century: central heating had been introduced, which allowed rooms to be opened up. And the railroad made it possible for a middle-class family to manage two houses. I admire those houses. They continue to define, for me, seaside life at its best. I first admired these houses because I had studied architecture at Yale with Vincent Scully, who wrote the book about that period. It was very much on our minds. I first thought all you needed to do was to make something shingled, and it would be Shingle Style. Now I don't think that's true. I think that the Shingle Style, with its roots in that vernacular tradition of New England houses, has a very specific character, very specific forms. And it's infinitely variable. Take one hundred architects and give them the same program, and turn them loose with the mandate to do it in the Shingle Style, and you will get one hundred different houses. You can even get one hundred different houses from one architect, because it is a language capable of infinite variation. I have looked seriously with what I would call a scholar's eye to see how these buildings are really made. And I have started to do houses, on Martha's Vineyard and Long Island and wherever else it seems appropriate, that I believe are successful extensions of that language; they belong to the tradition and to today.

167

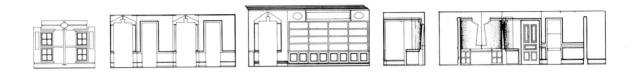

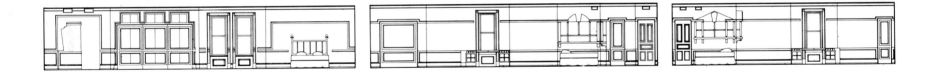

BLDD: *What leads you to move closer to history in some cases and further from it in others?*

RAMS: Like everyone else, I make judgments of situations. My judgments are based on my education and my experience in architecture, and my experience as a "real" person. I always feel that there are two kinds of people in the audience: there are my fellow professionals, whether they're interior designers or architects, and then there are real people—people who don't come with the whole baggage of prejudices that architects and designers have.

BLDD: *Are there rules or theories to your work? Or is it intuitive?*

RAMS: There are both, intuitions and rules.

BLDD: *What are some of the rules?*

RAMS: Rules are how you make a room.

BLDD: *How do you make a room? Where do you start— what's the most important thing in an interior?*

RAMS: I like to be able to get into the middle of a room and be able to look all different ways and sense a kind of orderly organization of the parts. Then I would like to sense that orderly organization contradicted by a second reading of a disorganization, of another relationship. I like a dialogue that can be enriching. But I like the basic context established, and then the change. I like rooms that have a decided floor quality. I don't like wall-to-wall carpeting particularly, because it doesn't have that quality. I think a pattern on the floor, in the wood, that reinforces the room's geometry, helps you to understand it. Similarly, if I had my choice I wouldn't have flat ceilings. They seem wrong to me. I like the volume of the ceiling to reinforce the centrality of the room. Why be in the center of the room, you might ask? Because I still believe that man is the center of all things on this earth. And one thing you want to do is get in the middle and be able to feel that you're more important than the room, that you are the ordering device. I like doors that are more than just holes in the wall; I like them to have some sort of treatment or elaboration around them. I like the door to my house to look different from the door to my refrigerator. The refrigerator door can be an industrial part, the door to my house should have the character, the particularity, of architecture. I don't like architecture as industrial design. We've had a generation of architecture which was based on industrial design.

BLDD: *Are you saying goodbye to high tech, or did you never say hello?*

RAMS: I never said hello to high tech. I don't know what high tech is. I use industrial things for themselves. I have a pencil sharpener in my house, and I have . . .

BLDD: *Things that facilitate your existence rather than embellish it?*

RAMS: Yes. They can be very beautiful, but I don't want to make a building look like a pencil sharpener. I am fascinated by this plain glass bowl and these flowers in the bowl. If we took the flowers out of the bowl, we wouldn't have much. Whereas, if we took the flowers out of a bowl from the Ming period, or any period in the history of art before the industrial process became the germinative source for form, we'd have a bowl which had a character in and of itself.

BLDD: *Do you think that fifty or one hundred years from now, one might look at a clear glass form and think that it accurately and historically represents the continuity of the classical vocabulary, and reflects this age?*

RAMS: No. It will reflect the impact of the obsession with machine production which characterized "progressive" or "advanced" or whatever you want to call the art of fifty years ago. Philip Johnson had a show at the Museum of Modern Art in 1933 in which he showed his industrial art and the machine. They were hot items then. They're not hot items any more.

BLDD: *There is certainly a dearth of craftsmanship.*

RAMS: You don't have craftsmanship because nobody asks the craftsmen. We have a Museum of Contemporary Crafts on Fifty-third Street in New York, in which the craftsmen make things that can't be used. They are never asked to make things to be used. You buy a vase in that museum, or in a crafts gallery, and the first thing they tell you is, "Don't put any water in it!" It's absolutely absurd.

BLDD: *What do you think of the state of American crafts?*

RAMS: It's lost all relationship to high art, because high art dismissed craft as just craft. Benvenuto Cellini was a craftsman, but he wasn't shown at a Museum of Contemporary Crafts back in Florence in the old days. He was operating in his way as part of an artistic tradition.

BLDD: *Does your office require the work of craftspersons?*

RAMS: We've been fortunate in finding amazing people who are thrilled to do things for us. Some we get from the decorating profession, I have to admit. We now know where to get people who can make the most beautiful marble out of plywood through the magic of paint.

BLDD: *What have they been doing for the last thirty years?*

RAMS: They've either been working for decorators, or they haven't been asked. Or they've worked on theater sets and things like that. Once we planned to do a stone fireplace in Maine, and we imagined that to do it we would have to sketch it and then make working drawings and all that stuff. We met the craftsman and showed him a rough sketch of what we wanted, and said, "We'll send you a drawing." He said, "Don't send me a drawing; I know what you want. And I'll do it." From that sketch he made an absolutely beautiful fireplace. He understood his material. We then asked him how often he did these things. He said he hadn't done one in years. And we asked, "Why?" He said, "Nobody asked." I guess nobody cares if their stone walls look like Pizza Huts.

Architects, artists and interior designers have tremendous power and want to exercise it in areas they know nothing about—sociology, subway planning, traffic planning, a million things. But their real power is in the artistic idea. An artistic idea that is rooted in tradition brings with it a tremendous authority. An idea that is rooted only in the moment or only

in technology has nothing, really, to do with art.

BLDD: *You've said that architecture is no longer an image of the world as the architect wishes it to be, but as it is. What happened to the idea of the architect as reformer or revolutionary?*

RAMS: I hope it went out with the dodo bird. I may be the most zealous reactionary or the most zealous revolutionary in my personal life. But my job as an architect is to take a situation and to translate it into a three-dimension thing we call a building, which not only can be used, but will also, in its design, represent that situation in relation to its tradition. We're not the first society to have had a democracy; we're certainly not the first society to have had troubles in our democracy; we're not the first society to have had wars. Yet why have we not been able to produce a war monument that's convincing in the last thirty years? Because we've tried to make war monuments look like bullets, or like lightening bolts. Gropius once designed one like that, and Mies did one that was just planes. They didn't mean anything.

BLDD: *Your kind of design cannot very often be found in the corporate world of large office buildings. Why do you think this is the case? Has modernism, which was once such a radical style, now become the ultimate conservative expression?*

RAMS: It's the perfect style for the man in the gray flannel suit. Once corporations had swagger, and Colonel McCormick wanted to emblazon his name and that of his company through the building. Now, typically—and probably quite correctly, given the hanky-panky in Detroit and everywhere else—each corporation wants to be more anonymous than the next. So I take my hat off to organizations like AT&T, that really have taken the plunge and continue the great tradition. I think things are changing. The buildings around New York, though they are largely still pretty dull, are much less dull than they once were.

169

Robert A. M. Stern
Apartment, interior elevation
1980

170

Robert A. M. Stern
Staircase
1979

Robert A. M. Stern
Study
1980

Robert A. M. Stern
Drawing for "Griffin" table
1981

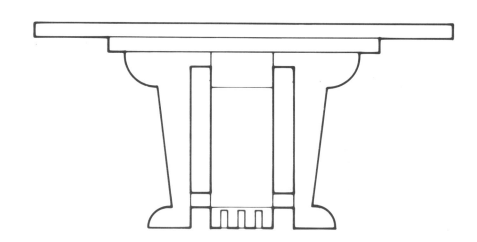

171

Robert A. M. Stern
Dining room
1980

Following pages:
Robert A. M. Stern
Poolhouse, interior and
exterior elevations

Robert A. M. Stern
"Temple of Love" bedroom
1979

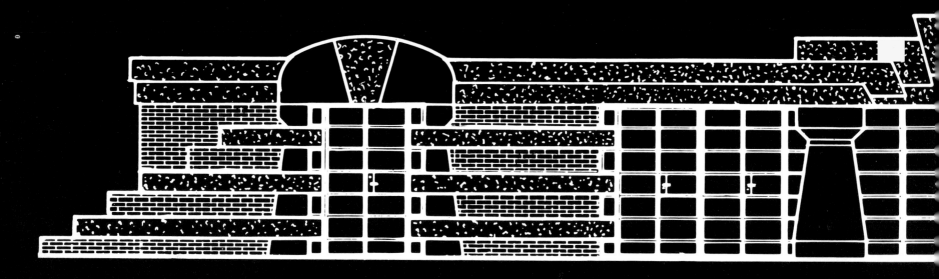

BLDD: *There is almost nothing that Lella and Massimo Vignelli haven't designed—furniture, glassware, flatware, exhibition layouts, books, posters, jewelry, furniture, corporate trademarks, store showrooms and interiors. The Vignellis are total designers, interested in shaping the whole environment. Is there anything that you exclude from your interests—anything that you* don't *design?*

MV: There is something: things with mechanisms. I can't understand them. If there is a mechanism—as in a typewriter, radio or bicycle—I stay away. I can only think as far as a hinge. A hinge is okay.

BLDD: *Is there anything that you haven't yet designed that you'd like to?*

LV: There are many things, especially from the standpoint of design for the home, and fashion. We feel that clothing is really an extension of design, if it's done in a different way—not as changing fashion, but lasting, as the designs we do now for graphics and furniture.

BLDD: *Have you ever designed clothing?*

LV: We have a concept for clothing. That's what we call it: "clothing concept." It's not fashion, in a sense. We still haven't found the right outlet. The idea, though, is not going to get old, because it is *not* fashionable.

MV: The role of fashion is transitory. The role of clothing is permanent. In all our design we are more interested in permanence than the transitory things that make fads, or fashions. "Fad," after all, is a derogatory term for a fashion. Our profession is greatly changed. We are interested in clothing. Nobody is taking care of clothing. The only decent clothes you find around are working clothes.

BLDD: *You referred to your idea as a concept. Are you saying that there is a philosophy that unites all the diverse work that you do, whether it is furniture or clothing?*

MV: I have three points I talk about all the time. The philosophy is: discipline, appropriateness and ambiguity.

BLDD: *Discipline, appropriateness and ambiguity—I under-* stand the first two qualities; they seem clear enough. But could you please expand on that last term—what do you mean when you say "ambiguity"?

MV: Ambiguity is that state where things contradict each other and are valid because that contradiction is there. They are valid because they are pushed to the extreme limit but they never go beyond it. It is a moment of tension, a moment neither here nor there. It's a beautiful state of mind and a terrific one. It's the moment of excitement, the moment of creation. And ambiguity is something which is indefinable as well.

LV: It's in the making.

MV: This is always there in our design. It's terrific. I love it. In the design for a recent table all the pieces in the base, except one, are standing up. One is lying down. Why is it lying down? Because by lying down it creates an ambiguous situation. It is evocative. Standing up is a metaphor for life. So with one piece lying down, the base of the table becomes an ambiguous thing. What is it doing there? It is suddenly taking away the simple geometry of those pieces and bringing to them history and life. That is the kind of thing we like. At the beginning we called it "Metaphora." It was first produced in Italy. Now that it is distributed in the United States, it's called "Euclid." It was the distributor's idea.

BLDD: *"Euclid" is probably a good reference to any of your work, because of its very strong underlying geometry.*

LV: Absolutely. Again, this is because geometry doesn't go out. It is not a fad, it's an eternal value. We always try to have a very strong geometry in our design. We don't go in for wavy lines or contours because we don't believe in that.

MV: This doesn't mean that everything should be primary geometry. It could be complex geometry. What I mean is total geometry. Nevertheless, it moves, it flows. It just happens that we like rather simple, pure geometry, again, because it is somehow easier to master.

BLDD: *What do you mean when you talk about "discipline"? Obviously, every profession requires discipline in its work.*

Lella & Massimo Vignelli

How do you apply that quality to the creative process?
MV: It's a methodological attitude. Discipline is a search for a structure in whatever you do—in our case, graphic structure, or three-dimensional structure. You have to have that kind of a discipline of structure in communication. That's why, by the way, my biggest partner is Webster's Dictionary. Every time we get a new job, we look in Webster's. The definition there most of the time keeps you on target. It helps you avoid going off on a tangent of misunderstanding.
BLDD: *Most of us think your biggest partner is Lella Vignelli! Your work together is probably the ultimate test of collaboration. You've been partners in work and in marriage for a quarter of a century. Why don't you tell us how this team effort works—who does what?*
MV: We both do everything. We discuss everything together, and then each of us more or less takes over his own follow-up. But we check continuously, and although Lella is more involved with three-dimensional things, and I'm more involved with graphics, I'm also involved with three-dimensional things and Lella is involved with graphics in the sense that we discuss whatever project we are doing. The attitude—and it is a very simple one—has always been that if Lella doesn't like it, it goes in the wastebasket. It's much easier to find a new design than to argue!
BLDD: *Someone told me that yours is really an alliance between the possible Massimo and the practical Lella.*
MV: Sure. It's much faster to do a new thing than to try to convince her!
LV: Massimo is very fast with ideas. But because he's fast, the ideas are sometimes vague, so they go in the basket. I feel that the most important thing, and it was perhaps not so clear or strong at the beginning, is that now we are really helping each other. We are not out any more to show who is best, who has the first idea, and so on. Some times years ago when we were more insecure, that was there. Now, instead, we are out to help each other, and so it is not just, "In the basket!" auto-

matically. We try to take the next step; we try to give the ideas consideration.
BLDD: *Is an idea ever retrieved from the basket?*
LV: Oh, yes. Sometimes it goes in a drawer because it is a terrific idea but not appropriate for the job.
BLDD: *Both of you studied architecture in Italy and in the United States. How did your work evolve from the built environment to the kind of work that you do now?*
LV: It was a natural step for somebody who was educated in Italy, because all the Italian design is made by architects.
MV: We have no school of design, you know. Italy, which is probably one of the leading countries for design in the world, has no design school.
LV: Now they're starting some, but nothing really serious. The architects still do everything.
BLDD: *The schools of architecture turn out a good number of graduates every year basis and everybody can't build buildings.*
MV: There are 7,000 students of architecture in Venice alone.
LV: Also, the curriculum always included interiors, scenography, furniture design and product design. So it was already structured in such a way that the architect should take care of all this.
BLDD: *As I recall, in your family, Lella, there are a lot of architects.*
LV: Right, there are a lot of architects. They are all involved with architecture and design. My father was the first, and then, out of four children, three are architects, married to architects. And now the grandchildren are in schools of architecture.
BLDD: *How do you contrast the architectural education in this country with that of Italy?*
LV: Schools here are much more on target architecturally. I was on a fellowship at MIT, and there the emphasis was not only on architecture but structural engineering, too, and not at all on design. Now it is starting, but years ago, no architect 177

would have dreamed of being involved in interior design. That was a fantasy.

MV: Even when they were out of work?

LV: Right. There was a moment, though, historically, when they were out of work, that they turned to furniture design—for example, Charles Eames, during the Depression. That was probably the only example. It's sad that he did it only because he didn't have any building to do.

BLDD: *Did you intend to be an architect?*

LV: My first idea was to become a journalist, but then everybody was an architect—I met Massimo and he said, "What do you mean? You're not becoming an architect?" He was already in architectural school and I was not. So I was a pushover for architectural school. When I went for my first interview here, at Skidmore, Owings & Merrill in Chicago, Bruce Graham said, "The only opening is in interiors." I said, "Fantastic, terrific." He thought that I would never consider accepting the position. It was a completely different attitude.

BLDD: *Don't you think that happens to some young women architects today, and that they are not as responsive to that suggestion as you were?*

LV: I don't know. But I think that now many architects, by designing their own interiors, are beginning to get more interested in them.

BLDD: *Do you think there is a greater emphasis on interior design and the total environment within architecture?*

LV: I think that a building is not finished without interiors—it's sort of crazy to let it go.

MV: The attitude of the architects has changed in that respect. They want to be more in total command of the entire project they are creating, so they design the building, they design the interiors, and they design the furniture.

BLDD: *How important is it to be aware of the past in terms of design?*

MV: Oh, extremely important. The past is the best thing that ever happened! You know, today is the past of tomorrow,

178

Massimo and Lella Vignelli
"Skyline" architecture and
design calendar
1978

that's what is so funny.

LV: And also, you can never invent anything. You just reinterpret, reuse a shape or a technique that was invented for something else in a new way. The more you know, the more creative you can be.

BLDD: *Why don't you tell us how you used an awareness of the past and an historical reference in one of the objects you've designed?*

MV: We had to do glasses for the CIGA Hotel chain in Venice. And I was sitting there at the great hotel, looking at the church of La Salute, which has a dome with ribs. The president of the company was saying, "How are our glasses going to be? Do you have any ideas?" And I said, "Like that dome. Exactly like that." It relates to Venice, it's a marvelous shape, and another thing, which is fun, is that a lot of forms become something else when you turn them upside down. Begin with a dome; turn it upside down and it becomes a glass. To look at the past with a kind of investigative eye or amusing eye is fun. It just makes it very familiar, very handy.

BLDD: *Is there a Vignelli look?*

MV: That would be the negation of all that we stand for. We don't want to have a look. I think when we do have a look, it's because our design is too weak. We are not interested in a personal style. We're not interested in a style as it has been classified. We are interested in raising the standard of design, and the more anonymous that is, the better it is, to a certain extent. But you need also the style. You need the peaks and the valleys. But we are not interested in being at either a peak or a valley—we are interested in raising the plateau.

BLDD: *There is, obviously, a Vignelli attitude.*

MV: That I like better. Attitude is a permanent thing. A style is a transitory thing, and I have no liking for transitory things.

BLDD: *How does your office work? How many people work with you and what do they do?*

MV: It works beautifully. Terrific! Twenty-five very good

designers working, having a lot of fun. Lella and I talk about the project, we call in one of the designers, we talk with him or her and then, generally speaking, the designer follows up, and we follow that, too.

LV: We have some sessions together to sort of break the problem and come out with ideas.

MV: We're very much on top of it.

BLDD: *How do you divide the work? Who does what?*

LV: As Massimo was saying before, if it's graphic, it is in his field; if it's three-dimensional, it's in my field, but you always cross over, really. There is also the designer. The great thing is that people who work with us really learn to cross boundaries, and even if they are graphic, they start to be interested in the three-dimensional. Or coming from the other side—the architects and product designers get into graphics to a certain extent.

MV: It's like a school, in a sense.

LV: They learn to have respect for a broader point of view, and field of activity.

BLDD: *Do you keep an idea file or do you design out of your own need, or do you work only by commission or assignment?*

LV: Generally it is by commission and assignment; when we do something by our own need, it is because we need it for ourselves. For example, the sofa that we designed in 1964—the Saratoga sofa that's still around—was done because we really needed a sofa for our house. That is the best way to design, because then you really do it right.

MV: We live out of our prototypes. We eat off of our dishes, we have our own flatware, glassware, furniture.

LV: Sometimes, for example, we design for a furniture company, which asks for chairs and a table. We have a couple of ideas, perhaps. They accept one; the other goes back in the drawer. There are ideas we are using now that we first had in 1971. They come out now as a piece of furniture.

BLDD: *I've rarely been in your company when something did not happen and you said, "Oh, that's a great idea." Do you*

then write it down somewhere, file it away, and retrieve it later?

LV: Absolutely.

BLDD: *Has there been a recent example of the use of something from that file that you've applied on a practical and manufactured basis? How about the new Kyoto line of lacquerware that you've done—"the clean pile of dirty dishes"?*

MV: It's an amusing story. When you serve dinner, you have the table all set up, the candles and the plates and the crystal and flatware and the whole thing. It's beautiful. You sit down, and you start eating, talking, eating and drinking, talking, eating and drinking and, gradually, you are moving the whole table toward the garbage can. It becomes an awful mess. Finally, at the end, since we have no butlers around, you have that awful job of collecting the dishes and picking up the flatware along with the leftover chicken bones and all those things, you know . . .

LV: You make it so disgusting!

MV: I want to make it disgusting because it is a disgusting thing. We said, "We have to design backwards."

BLDD: *Won't you tell us how you transformed that idea, from your need and philosophy and attitude, into a reality—how did it end up being these dishes?*

MV: In this case, we designed it from the end, from the time when the leftovers are there. What you do is take your flatware, you put it inside, and it stays there. Then you take another dish, and you put the one on top of the other. You don't have to get the flatware out. You don't have to put your fingers on it. You just make a whole pile of dishes by taking each one and putting it on top of the others, and you have a clean pile of dirty dishes—which is quite an achievement.

BLDD: *You have been experimenting and designing with plastic material for quite some time. There is hardly a household, regardless of economic range or geographical location, that doesn't have some of your plastic tableware that comes in rainbow colors. When did you first do that?*

MV: That was done in 1964. We were doing a project for a small company which was in the plastic business, and one of the partners had another small company which was making Mickey Mouse ashtrays. And I said, "If you can make that, how about making a set of dinnerware which would be stackable, very compact and nice? Maybe we can win a nice design award." I *wanted* to win a design award. Anything which could get me that would have been good. So I had the idea, went back to the office, and half an hour later we had the whole thing. And we came out in production in a month and a half.

LV: In two months. We got the award, by the way!

BLDD: You also got a lot of imitations of that design.

MV: Oh, everything. That's the only sad thing—financially it's the sad thing, because they preempt your own market.

BLDD: *Don't you patent your designs?*

MV: We want to raise the standards—that's the first thing.

LV: Now we patent our designs, but at that point, we didn't really know and often we didn't patent it. That first Hellerware design was *not* patented, not even the handle, which in a sense was another breakthrough, because that particular handle was not around before. Now you see it in innumerable imitations. Everywhere. On everything.

BLDD: *But you've learned...*

MV: We started to do ads for Sotheby-Parke Bernet, the auction house. The design had paper with thick lines separating every category of sale. It was very strong, terrific.

BLDD: *Which is, if I may say so, very typical of the Vignelli graphic style, where very strong horizontals are emphasized.*

MV: Sure enough, Christie's, the other auction house, had announcements printed with very thin lines, and now every week they are thickening and gasping for air. Finally it will come out all the same, and will probably preempt our Sotheby image. Sotheby's will say, "Everybody is doing it like us, we've got to do something else." But they should keep doing that. The followers are the first ones to get tired, by the way.

BLDD: *For whom is this plastic tableware designed, both the Heller line—which I assume is more modest in cost—and this almost lacquer-look plasticware?*

LV: This new one is for an Italian company, but is going to be distributed here in the United States. The first store that will have it is Barney's clothing store in New York.

BLDD: *Were your designs for the decanter, the two glasses and the flatware all done for commercial rather than residential purposes? How do you make that distinction? Why couldn't any one of those products be used at home?*

MV: As a matter of fact, it's the same thing. For the CIGA Hotel chain, we designed the whole corporate identity: then they asked us to design china, glass and silverware. This is usually the story. Then we said, "By the way, your office needs a little re-doing," and then they said, "Well, you have done my office—how about doing my apartment?" It keeps going on. The flatware was done for them and so everything relates to that theme, and those lines. But it is also available on the market, for private use. It is silver-plated.

LV: The only difference really is a technical one. The silver-plating is much heavier on the CIGA flatware in order to stand up under the rough use, but the function of the object doesn't change.

MV: First we designed the flatware and the glassware. But then one day I went to Venice to present these things and I came up with about a dozen other items, including a nutcracker. The manufacturer was there and so in a couple of hours we had to design all those things—really one sketch after the other. The manufacturer said, "I like the look of this." And it was done just like that: we gave the sketches to this manufacturer and they immediately went into production. This is part of the fun of our design, that it's fast.

BLDD: *Other than your own apartment, are there any interiors that you do?*

LV: Not for private clients.

LV: Interiors can be terribly time-consuming, so we elected to

do them only for companies or institutions like museums or churches. They are different from an office.

BLDD: *Did you ever do a house?*

MV: I did a house when I was in school, and it was too much work. Besides, it was not as much fun as graphics and design, which is quick and you can see right away whether it comes out right or wrong. With a house, you have to wait all that time to get it constructed and then if it is wrong, you've got to find another client, to build another house, which is going to take another long time.

BLDD: *How do you find your clients?*

MV: They come by themselves, thank God. That's no problem.

BLDD: *You designed an apartment for yourselves not too long ago on the Upper East Side of Manhattan. What does the interior of your own apartment look like?*

LV: It is very spare. As a matter of fact, some time ago a lady came in and said, "I understand you would like a few more things around, wouldn't you?" And I was so taken aback by her not understanding that I didn't even dare to say no. I said, "Oh yes, yes. Naturally."

BLDD: *Why do you want it to look the way it does?*

LV: First, because all the things that are around should be perfect, so we only buy the few things that we can afford at the time. We don't like collectibles.

MV: Collecting junk takes too much room. Collecting good things takes too much money. So we are caught in between. We can't do it.

BLDD: *But you do collect your own designs in that apartment, including some early designs—such as the Saratoga chair, that goes back about seventeen years. Can you describe what the Saratoga chair looks like?*

MV: It's just like a wall, basically. It's a square box, lacquered like a piano. Suppose you take a square piano and then you put a seat on it: that's what the Saratoga looks like.

BLDD: *More like a piano bench?*

MV: It's very boxy and it's black lacquer.

LV: One interesting thing about that design is that the back and the arms are, as we say, boxy, lacquered, and six inches wide—which, in 1964, were enormous. That thing looked so big! "The fat chair," as Angelo Donghia has said. Now those are the normal dimensions because furniture is becoming bigger and bigger.

MV: And the houses are becoming smaller and smaller. Soon they will be filled in completely.

BLDD: *You have an office here and in Italy as well. What are the most dramatic changes that you've observed in the years since your design office opened here?*

MV: I think the improvement is sensational. When we came over here fifteen years ago, everything was just ugly. Everything. It was unbelievable. There was not a good chair on the market besides the Mies and Eames chairs, or antique chairs, of course. It was like that for some time. The only good things were imported from Europe.

BLDD: *There was a time there that we were beginning to think that Italy was the design center of the world, but that doesn't seem to be the case any longer.*

MV: No, and this is terrific. Now you have places like Conran's, you have places like the Pottery Barn, you have places like the Workbench.

BLDD: *You're referring to stores that make available at modest prices things of genuine quality and design.*

MV: You've also got the department stores. These places didn't sell inexpensive, well-designed things fifteen years ago. Now there is an explosion of good things at affordable prices, which really is the most important thing—young people do not want to live with the same junk that the previous generation wanted.

BLDD: *That's encouraging.*

MV: Of course. Thank God we did something. I think we all did something—not only ourselves, but we have been preaching design. Really that is what we have done for the last twenty-five years.

181

*Massimo and Lella Vignelli
Saks Fifth Avenue packaging
1979*

*Massimo and Lella Vignelli
Bloomingdale's packaging
1972*

BLDD: *How has your work been affected by this new aware-ness, and the availability of things at affordable prices?*
MV: Heller was the one who was in the business for good design at affordable prices. That's what he wanted to do, and I liked the idea. I think it's important. I think the opposite is also important, however. I love precious materials and noble materials, and I can't stand certain others.
BLDD: *Which materials can't you bear?*
MV: Certain kinds of plastic materials; materials which imi-tate others. I love Formica if you use it as Formica, but I don't like it when you use it as wood, things like that.
BLDD: *You're very philosophical, you're informed by the past and you talk about raising the standard of design. In the end, do you feel that design really can improve society? Is it an act that has real social meaning or is it more a question of designing beautiful things for people who can afford to pay for them?*
MV: I must tell you that fifteen years ago I was convinced you could transform or at least help to transform society with good design. I know now that good design does not transform society. The only thing that transforms society is economic power. We all agree about that. Nevertheless, design could make your micro-environment look much better than it looks now. The architect takes care of the macro-environment, the politician takes care of this country, which is the supermacro-environment. The politician takes care of the nation. That's the supermacro. The planner and the architects take care of the macro-environment—regions, cities, buildings.
BLDD: *And what are we responsible for?*
MV: We take care of the micro-environment. But I think that the micro-environment is the world which is all around us, all the time, until we go out to the streets. We are continuously surrounded by furniture, objects, desks, pens, things like that. That is the micro-environment. Generally speaking, the qual-ity of the micro-environment was terrible before and it's now getting much better. The other day someone showed me a Tif-

fany pen clip that's now coming out. It is a beautiful, simple design. It's not the kind of pen clip I would design, but it was an object which I enjoyed. It's fine, a super design, and it's modestly priced. It's great. These things were not available fif-teen years ago. Now places like Tiffany, which was the temple of conformity, are coming up with good designs all the time.
BLDD: *Isn't that another kind of conformism—if we didn't know that a well-known designer was attached to that design, might it be such a success?*
LV: There is a little of that here. In Europe there is a lot of that—the name of the designer has snob appeal, which did not used to be true here at all. But now it is starting a little.
MV: In Italy designers are as famous as movie actors. Every-body knows Gae Aulenti in Italy, just as they know Sophia Loren, for different reasons. But, it's terrific. They know all about it.
BLDD: *How do you compare the state of Italian design and American design today?*
LV: In Italy it is much more diffused. Here it's just starting, so we have very few objects that are "designer," and fewer companies that are involved. The future of design is here because more and more companies are beginning to call on designers, which they were not doing years ago. The situation, naturally, is much bigger here and it will take a longer time to complete the circle, as it happened in Italy.
BLDD: *Looking back, do you think your career would have been any different if you had remained in Italy rather than coming here? I'm specifically asking you that not only as someone who came from Italy, but as a woman, as well.*
LV: In a sense, my career would have been faster in Italy.
BLDD: *Because of your family involvement?*
LV: No, no. But for a professional woman there was immedi-ate recognition. There was no difference between a woman and a man; it was not even considered a problem. Here, it was.
BLDD: *Was that because there were fewer professional women in Italy?*

182

Massimo and Lella Vignelli
Goblets
1979

Massimo and Lella Vignelli
Flatware and nutcracker
1979

LV: Exactly. So if you became professional, there was just no question. Here, instead, there was the fact that you were a woman. And for quite a long time there really was a different way of treating women.

BLDD: *And now, twenty years later?*

LV: No, I wouldn't say there is now. But perhaps I conquered all, so my position, personally, is not to be intimidated by the situation or by certain attitudes. I would have been recognized faster in Italy, but certainly it would have been on a smaller scale; the great thing about working here is the sense of scale and the sense of power that you get. And also the sense of security—because in Italy things go very fast, but it's a country of prototypes, so you have a lot of prototypes, you have your name all over the place. Here it takes a longer time but you are really on more solid ground, I think.

MV: The point is this: here, the industry is addressing itself to a nation of two hundred and twenty million people. Unless the manufacturers get the whole market, they are not interested in producing something. This is wrong, because even ten per-cent of that market is bigger than all the European markets put together. It's a matter of attitude, but it's coming along.

BLDD: *You mentioned earlier raising the level of design acceptance by the public. But is there any mass marketer of furniture that employs the service of a well-known designer?*

LV: They are really just starting in the mass market. It will come in the next few years.

BLDD: *You have redesigned many very standard things. And I've often wondered if there are some objects that really can't be improved upon. For example, could anyone design a better spoon?*

MV: Not really.

BLDD: *Do you think that some things can be made to look too new?*

MV: There are different aspects of an object. There are functional aspects and there are aspects of communication. The communication aspects are more transitory because the levels of message get more or less articulate with time. The communicative aspect of a spoon relates to a very wide field. But the functional aspect of a spoon only relates to your mouth, and that's been pretty much the same for the last couple of billion years. So it's kind of easy in that respect. There is no great improvement there, but there is a lot of improvement in the decorative part, if you want to call it that.

BLDD: *What new ground are you considering breaking these days? What do you see as the future direction and emphasis of your work?*

LV: From my point of view, I see more furniture and product design. Manufacturers are also becoming more aware of design and more aware of what they need from the designer, so I hope that that will be a natural direction.

MV: Another interesting area is work with other artists. We have designed a table now whose legs have been done by a sculptor. The shape is our four cylinder table.

BLDD: *Why don't you describe what the table looks like?*

MV: The table is a slab, resting on four cylinders, with a corner cut out. Normally it is produced in wood. But now we have done another version where the four cylinders, which are basically four columns, are done by Arnaldo Pomodoro, the sculptor, who usually creates forms within a geometric shape.

LV: It is a very interesting possibility—to collaborate with artists—and we would like to do more in that direction. Really, it's working together with an artist who is on the same wave length. Pomodoro was a natural.

MV: We'd also like to do flatware and plates with him.

BLDD: *I know the whole subject of collaboration between artists and architects is one that is very close to you and one to which you've given considerable thought.*

LV: Again, it goes back to history, and new research in design as it was historically.

MV: For instance, we had designed some teapots. One teapot is rather amusing. It's a pyramid, in silver, and the handle and spout is a snake which penetrates and comes out on the

183

other side. The snake is done as in the Renaissance.

LV: It's a reinterpretation, a new point of view.

BLDD: *One of your most unusual and demanding assignments was to design the furnishings for St. Peter's Church, that sort of giant paperweight tucked into the Citicorp building in New York. How did that assignment come about?*

MV: They called and said, "We'd like you to design the interior of St. Peter's." I said, "Well, it's about time!" Of course I was thinking of St. Peter's in Rome. Then I found out what it was. There are plenty of good designers in the world, but very few good clients, and Pastor Peterson of St. Peter's was one of the few.

BLDD: *What is a "good" client?*

MV: A client with understanding, to begin with, and a client who has no fear . . .

LV: In that case, a client who doesn't ask you, "Did you ever design a church before?" He didn't ask that question. No, no.

BLDD: *What did you do for the church?*

LV: It was not just a church but really a meeting hall and a concert hall as well as a ministry. So the design had to accomplish all this. When we were talking with the pastor and the interiors committee and trying to define what the space should be, since it was not a traditional space, we finally came up with the definition: it should be a *moral* space. This was a perfect definition of what the space should be.

BLDD: *What is a moral space?*

MV: We didn't want it to smell of incense all the time because it would have been out of place for a concert or for a ballet or a theater performance. And we didn't want it to look much like a theater because it would have been out of place for a funeral or a wedding, or a religious service. So it had to be a very ambiguous, very flexible kind of place. The only thing which could be consistent was a certain moral quality about the space and the materials. One time Lella explained what we intended for "moral space." She said, "Just the opposite of a catering palace."

BLDD: *What did you do specifically for that interior? What materials did you use?*

LV: The materials, naturally, are sort of noble and long-lasting—like granite, and solid oak, and a very thick strong natural linen, and the wool that they used for the petit point. We chose to use solid oak and not veneer because we really wanted the pews to be as long-lasting and heavy as the pews of a traditional church. We chose also to go with pews because we didn't want to have a forest of chair legs. To define them architecturally, the space occupied by the sitting units is like that in colonial New England churches, sort of boxy. And all the steps around the church, which are really part of the architecture when they are closed, can open up and become seats. We didn't want to have a sea of empty seats when there are few people in the church.

MV: That could be very depressing.

LV: The other element that is particular to the design of this space is that there are a lot of modular platforms and steps to form the elevation of the altar that can be moved around in different positions, from the center to one side or to the other, to change it completely from a central church to a long nave church. So although everything has a permanent look, it is designed so it is modular and mobile.

BLDD: *In this moral space, why are there no crosses?*

MV: Again, there are no crosses because of the flexibility of use. You don't want to be obsessed all the time by a cross there. The cross becomes a very interesting part of the ceremony; when the whole procession of the clergy comes out before the service, they plant the cross on the platform of the altar. In that moment, and only in that moment, that place becomes a church, just as the forest becomes a forest in the Elizabethan theater, with just one plant. It's a beautiful, powerful image. . .

184

Massimo and Lella Vignelli
"Saratoga" furniture
1964

Massimo and Lella Vignelli
"Circolo" sofa and chair
1979

Massimo and Lella Vignelli
"Euclid" coffee table
1979

Following page:
Massimo and Lella Vignelli
Interior, St. Peter's Church
New York, N.Y.
1977

Massimo and Lella Vignelli
Stackable cups and saucers
1970

Massimo and Lella Vignelli
Glass micro/ovenware
1975

Next page:
Massimo and Lella Vignelli
Hauserman showroom
Los Angeles
1982

Photographic Acknowledgments

Aaron, Peter (Esto): 26–27, 30–31, 44, 45, 89, 147, 153, 154, 156, 157
Ardiles Arce, Jaime: 34, 41, 42, 43, 46–47, 155
Ballo, Aldo: 185
Barnes, Rick: 92, 93, 94–95
Beadle, Ernst: 60
Carrieri, Mario: 188, 189
Champion, Richard: 39, 59
Cserna, George: 186
David-Edward Ltd. (Ron Solomon): 148, 149
Dunne, Michael: 124
Georges, Alexandre: 118, 125
Kolleogy, Frank: 50, 53, 62, 63
McGrath, Norman: 37, 87
Molesworth, Greg: 115
Paige, Peter: 126, 127
Pàteman, Michael: 18, 21, 25, 28–29
Pellegrini, Frances: 61
Stoecklein, Ed: 170, 174–175
Stoller, Ezra (Esto): 130, 133, 136, 138–139
Tomlinson, Doug: 88
Vignelli, Luca: 185
Vitale, Peter: 90, 91, 158–159
Yoshimi, Toshi: 190
Zane, Steve: 121, 122, 123